FORGIVEN FOREVER

FORGIVEN FOREVER

the FULL FORCE *of* GOD'S TENDER MERCY

JOE BEAM

HOWARD
PUBLISHING CO.

Our purpose at Howard Publishing is to:

- *Increase faith* in the hearts of growing Christians
- *Inspire holiness* in the lives of believers
- *Instill hope* in the hearts of struggling people
  everywhere

Because He's coming again!

Published by Howard Publishing Co., Inc.
3117 North 7th Street, West Monroe, Louisiana 71291-2227

98 99 00 01 02 03 04 05 06 07   10 9 8 7 6 5 4 3 2 1

Library of Congress Cataloging-in-Publication Data

Beam, Joe.
    Forgiven forever : the full force of God's tender mercy / Joe Beam.
      p.   cm.
    Includes bibliographical references.
    ISBN 1-878990-66-7
    1. Forgiveness of sin. I. Title.
    BT795.B2944 1998
    234' .5—dc21
                          98-13486
                          CIP

Interior design by LinDee Loveland
Manuscript editing by Philis Boultinghouse and Kay Marshall Strom

Scripture quotations not otherwise marked are from the New International Version (NIV) © 1973, 1978, 1984 by International Bible Society. Used by permission Zondervan Bible Publishers. Other Scriptures quoted from the King James Version (KJV) © 1961 The National Publishing Co.; the New American Standard Bible (NASB) © 1960, 1962, 1963, 1968, 1971, 1972, 1973 The Lockman Foundation.

This study is dedicated to

JIMMY ALLEN

This gifted revivalist and Bible teacher
opened my eyes—and the eyes of
multiplied thousands of others—to
the grace and mercy of God. He will
always be a spiritual hero whose godly
example of faith, dedication, and
courage I will try to follow.

☙

CONTENTS

CONTENTS

SETTING
the
STAGE

❧

My Story

I am a prodigal returned.

I'm proud of that.

And ashamed.

I glory in it even as I slump into spiritual depression by forcing myself to remember it. If you've ever been a prodigal, you understand the contradictory emotions tearing at my heart and mind just with the writing of the word. If you never have been, I don't know that I can explain. But I'll try.

You may remember the story of the prodigal son that Jesus told in the fifteenth chapter of Luke. You know the young man who had everything a young man could want but left it for a life of sin. Doesn't make much sense if you think about it logically. A wonderful home. Loving father. Riches and comfort and peace. Who knows why he left all that, why he abandoned all that was good and holy for a world of decadence and personal humiliation. You might think, "Well, he knows. The prodigal son knows why he left." But we who are prodigals would beg to disagree. He undoubtedly would know the details of *what* happened. Asking him to explain *why* they happened—especially why he did what he did—might prove altogether a different proposition. A much tougher task.

I know it would be for me.

In 1967 I enrolled as a freshman at a small Bible college in Montgomery, Alabama. Too young in years and too new to Christ, I had no idea why I was there. If you'd asked me at the time, I would have told you about my girlfriend dumping me and my preacher, Charles Mullins, convincing me to leave town for a few months. "Go to a Christian college," he urged, "and forget about her. Build a new life." I went, but I expected to be back home soon. I carried no desire for a Bible education, just a jealous lover sorrowfully begging for my return. Three months or less and I figured I'd be home, engaged.

Apparently God had something else in mind.

Within months of my arrival on campus and my immersion into an intensely Christian environment, I discovered the path God wanted for my life. I would be a preacher. To my great surprise, I learned that God had gifted me for it. Paul Tarence, one of my professors, allowed God to use him to mentor me. Between God and His servant, Paul, I was placed on the fast track. Within two years I married Alice Hilyer from Tallassee, Alabama, and was off to my first ministerial assignment in LaGrange, Georgia. I finished the last two years of my Bible degree by driving back and forth to Montgomery for classes while ministering to a gentle, small-town church willing to settle for a wet-behind-the-ears greenhorn. Why would they agree to such an arrangement? They said, "You're a boy, full of a boy's foolishness, but when you step into the pulpit, God makes you into a powerful man."

Heady stuff for a twenty-year-old.

It was almost as if God had placed a proverbial preaching silver spoon in my mouth. Doors opened, accolades came, more doors opened, and God blessed my ministry beyond my wildest dreams. Before too long I was speaking across America in revivals, youth gatherings, and Bible lectureships. After a few years, larger churches began to call. I even served as a full-time minister to a few of those larger churches. The last two grew rapidly in the short span I worked with them.

But my ministry was nearing its end.

In December 1979 I began ministering to a growing, exciting church back in Montgomery, the very city where God led me into ministry. I moved there after ministering three years for a growing church in Evansville, Indiana. Young, experienced, on fire, and ready to climb every mountain, I had become a highly marketable product to energetic churches yearning to reach the lost. In one meeting, a group of ministers described me as "the rising young star on the brotherhood horizon."

The problem was that I believed it.

Oh, please, don't misunderstand. I did love Jesus. My heart was tuned to Him, and my loyalty to Him was as sincere as a saint who would rather burn at the stake than deny his faith. I knew God through my Lord Jesus, and God knew me. I had the Father/child relationship with Him that Christians enjoy. But I know now, from this vantage point of life, that the relationship I had with God had its flaws. I depended too much on my ability and not enough on Him. Thought too highly of my gift. Enjoyed too much the praise that came with the position, rather than ceaselessly praising the One who gave it to me.

You might say I focused on the wrong things. Things I was about to lose.

What happened?

I can clearly describe for you the *how* and the *what*. I'm not yet sure I understand all of the *why*. All those years ago and I still wonder about the why. The short version is that I sank into a cesspool of sin. My sin. My fault. No one else's but mine. But that's not how I would have described it at the time.

How could a man who preached *against* sin and *for* a life surrendered to Jesus live in such contradiction to the words he proclaimed Sunday after Sunday? It didn't happen easily, nor did it happen overnight. Since those days I've learned a great deal more about our enemy, Satan, and the tactics he uses.[1] Unfortunately, I didn't take him or his forces so seriously in those days. Like an unaware rabbit, I carelessly allowed myself into the rattler's striking distance and paid the penalty for my foolishness.

What was my sin? What did I do?

Does it matter?

Any number of sins can lead a prodigal from his Father's home—gambling, drunkenness, adultery, homosexuality, thievery, and a host of others. Pick the sin that tempts you most. Even if that's not the one I committed, the process will be the same. I had a weakness, a need, that went unheeded and unfulfilled. Satan's wily forces placed an opportunity for satisfying that need before me. Oh, not blatantly. I was too strong for that. Slowly, subtly, seductively, they lured me in, taking great care not to raise the hackles of my spiritual defenses until I was well entrapped. Then, it was too late. When I finally admitted to myself where I was and what I'd done, I didn't have the strength to free myself. No, I didn't call for help. Who can a preacher tell his sins to without fear of losing his church? His reputation? His livelihood?

For me, there was no one.

At least no one who could rescue me.

I felt free to confide only in those who were becoming part of the sin, wholly or peripherally. My fate was set, though I prayed regularly for deliverance. Surely God answered those prayers. But soon after I would beg Him to help me stop, I would find myself enthralled and enmeshed. I have no doubt He sent the way out, the help, the deliverance. But as much as I meant it when I cried for His hand, I ignored it when face to face with the delirium of my sin. The wanting I felt while praying was no match for the wanting I felt when overpowered by the presence of the temptation.

The sin captured my mind and was well on its way to capturing my spirit. Guilt cascaded over me with the volume and force of a Niagara. Unable to cope with the shame and unable to free myself from the sin, I stumbled into other sins that hinted relief for my savaged soul—other counterfeit solutions for the unfulfilled cravings deep within my soul. I started to drink. Heavily. Hiding it from my wife and children. Hiding from my church and friends. Trying to hide myself from me.

Can you imagine the contempt I felt for myself when I would stand in a pulpit on Sunday morning, nursing a hangover no one knew I had, wishing I could believe the same things I was teaching people in the audience to believe? No, I think that if you haven't been there, you can't. Other prodigals can. Even non-preacher prodigals. They know what it is to loathe themselves while putting on the correct face for others to see.

Of course, it was only a matter of time until I was caught. In October of 1983, the church in Montgomery quietly fired me, and rightly so. My ministry, whatever it was supposed to have been, ended a little more than two months shy of its fourteenth anniversary. The church let me go as gently as they could, trying not to cause any more pain to me or my family than necessary. The leaders needed to protect the flock, and they did it the best way they knew how.

My marriage fared little better: Almost immediately, I left my wife and moved to another city. My marriage ended almost exactly on its fifteenth anniversary.

My life, for all practical purposes, was over.

I tried my best to forget about God.

And I especially tried to forget those "self-righteous, judgmental" church people.

No, that's not what they were. But in my spiritual condition, what else could I think about them? Could they have helped me more? Sure, if only they had known how. Should they have? From my prejudiced perspective, I definitely believe so. Abandoning one who is entrapped in sin is a cruel act. Someone said the church is the only army that shoots its wounded. Whoever said that hasn't ever been seriously wounded. The church doesn't shoot its wounded; shooting a wounded person could be viewed as an act of compassion. At least he won't suffer anymore. No, far too many churches pull the wounded to the side of the road and continue on their way, ignoring the wounded believer's cries of pain. They don't shoot them; they just abandon them to fend for themselves at the very time they have the least ability to do so.

Am I angry?

No, not at all. I haven't a doubt that those good folks did all they knew to do. They just didn't know enough.

That's why I'm writing this book.

You've seen that my life spiraled into the muck of a modern-day pigpen. Like the prodigal of Luke 15, I did more than leave the joy of my Father's house, I descended into a man-made hell. I was the man who made it.

Living a hundred miles from Montgomery, I divorced my wife. I also started a new business, a house-building business. As you might imagine, I had no clue how to build a house since I'd done nothing in my adult life but be a minister. Ignorantly, I figured I could hire people to build the houses, having great confidence in my ability to sell them.

We went bankrupt.

Within a year I had no money, no family, no church, and no job. Too proud to flip hamburgers, I held out for some executive position. Three factors kept me from getting such a position. First, I hadn't the training or experience. Second, my desperation made me as repulsive to interviewers as beer at a Baptist picnic. Third, when Christians discovered that I was interviewing at their company, they went out of their ways to advise the personnel department of my unsavory character.

Before long, I was without a place to live or food to eat. Ejected from my apartment for lack of rent payment, I lived in my car for a while. Sometimes I would go three days or more with nothing to eat because I hadn't the money to buy food. If I got my hands on ten dollars, I put it in my gas tank so I could keep looking for work. Sure, I could have asked any number of churches for help, but I was too proud, too angry, and too deluded by my own spiritual decay.

Oh, I went to church every Sunday. Habits die hard. And I still loved God, though I was very, very angry with Him. As if all of my mess was His fault or something.

Only when a Christian couple, the Crockers, encouraged me into a basement room just off their garage did I have opportunity to eat again with any regularity. But by then, it was too late. I wasn't hungry much anymore. I'd already discovered a new dimension that hadn't been part of my life before.

Nightclubs.

Bright lights on the outside that screamed "fun and frivolity" and dark lights on the inside so that things were whatever you wished them to be. Definitely the kind of place that appealed to my mental state. I didn't have any money, but I didn't need any. I discovered that if you knew a lot of jokes, people would buy you something to drink.

And I knew lots of jokes.

That got me a lot of liquor. Hanging out in the nightclubs did more than that for me—several bad things, some of which I just can't mention here. Can't stand to remember. But one of them was drugs.

When you sit in a bar, telling jokes and drinking, depression incongruously dripping from every pore, you attract attention. After a while someone comes by and says, "Hey, man. You're just too down. Here, take this." The person hands you some pill, and if you hurt badly enough, you don't even ask what it is. If it promises any relief from the overwhelming sadness, the pain, you just gulp it with a shot of vodka. If it gets you too high, someone else will come by. "Whoa, man. You're bouncing! You need to come down a little. Here, take this." You don't even look at it. For all you know it could have a skull and crossbones on it. What difference does it make? If it stops the pain, take it. You gulp it down with another shot of vodka.

Finally, you learn to visit people's bathrooms if they invite you to their houses and peek into their medicines. Find the right stuff, pocket it. Take it when you get the chance. Maybe tonight when you're drinking.

Do that enough, and it will *kill* you.

My second trip to the hospital in a few weeks' span was the night they told me I was going to die. Maybe the first trip made me overconfident. It was too easy for them to get the poison out of me and send me on my way. This time, I'd ingested too much. When the emergency-room physician realized the danger I was in, he asked if I knew any doctors in town. I thought of Dr. Frank Sutton, a pulmonary specialist, who is a wonderful Christian man. His specialty, of course, had nothing to do with the drugs being digested in my stomach and coursing through my veins, but I knew he would come. I knew he had the love of Jesus. I knew he was a Christian I could ask for help who wouldn't abandon me.

They dragged him from his bed, got him to the emergency room, filled him in, and brought him to me. I'll never forget the anger in his eyes and steel in his voice when he said, "You're at L 50." I asked what that meant. "Fifty percent of the people with this much in them die. You have a fifty-fifty chance of being alive in the morning."

No, I didn't react negatively to his anger. I knew it was because he loved me and because he felt so frustrated because there was little he could do. I'd have felt the same way if I were he.

The nurses had pumped my stomach shortly after my arrival, and now they wheeled me into intensive care. I watched dully as they rolled the defibrillator to my door and assembled a team for the anticipated code blue. They expected my heart to stop; they were gearing up to battle for my life.

The intensive-care nurse assigned to me never left my side. She held my hand, only releasing it to do some essential chore, then taking it again. Just the touch of a human helped. Her hand became my lifeline, my contact with care, my hope for someone loving me enough to fight for me.

Somewhere about daylight, she finally spoke other than for medical reasons. Softly, holding my hand, she asked the question that must have flirted with her mind all night, "Did you mean to kill yourself?"

I had to think before I answered.

"I don't think so. I mean, I don't want to die. I'm just not sure I want to live."

All I could think of was what a mess I'd made of my life, how I wished I could start over, how I longed for God to erase all the terrible things I'd done. Now that she asked, I felt that, maybe, I could talk with her. Tell her my pain. Get someone to understand.

"You know, I used to be a preacher . . ."

That's as far as I got. She released my hand, stepped back, and glared at me with intense hatred. Whatever button I'd pushed, it was major. With one last look of disgust, she spun and marched out my door. Never came back. Never. They had to scramble to find a nurse who would care for me.

I lay there thinking, "I've made such a mess of my life that I'm going to die alone. Even a nurse, an 'angel of mercy' won't help me. When you die a miserable sinner, you die completely abandoned . . . no one will even hold your hand."

After some time, vacillating between self-pity and self-loathing, I turned to God in heaven, the same God I had been crying out to in fear all night, begging Him not to punish me. I made Him the most important promise of my life. I prayed, "God, I have nothing to bargain with. Nothing to offer. But I'm dying a fool's death. If, in Your great mercy, You can somehow see fit to let me live, I promise You this: I'll spend the rest of my life learning how to die right."

At that moment, my life began to change. No, not miraculously. No angel appeared and held my hand. I didn't get up and walk out of there completely healed from my binge. My healing would take a couple more years to be complete. But it started there.

I finally learned what it is to live in the grace and mercy of God.

He gave me my wife and children back. Alice and I remarried in June of 1987, just three years after our divorce. We've even had a celebration child since then, Kimberly. She's eight as I write this.

And I learned how God heals prodigals like me. Prodigals who never will be comfortable with the knowledge of what they have done. Prodigals who will always be ashamed of the sins they've committed. Prodigals who rejoice in the forgiveness of God and have come to a level of relationship with Him where neither He nor they ever bring those sins into any remembrance between them.

If you are a prodigal, I hope to show you how God will bring you back. If you are a brother or sister to a prodigal, you should learn how God views prodigals and His message of hope to them. If you are a prodigal returned, you will find a peace you may have been fruitlessly searching for.

How can I promise these things?

Remember, I'm a prodigal returned.

That's what I want to teach you in this book. How God healed this prodigal.

And how God can heal you.

INTRODUCTION

Central casting couldn't have found anyone more grandmotherly than the lady standing before me. Soft curves of young womanhood had long since been overlaid with layers of coconut cake and pecan pie. She greeted me with that sweet, shy smile elderly women adopt when they aren't sure of themselves and asked if she could bother me for just a moment. I noted the smile but found a clearer message in the tears filling her eyes.

I didn't know what she wanted or what I could do to help. What wisdom could I possibly share with this crying, smiling woman, who was older than my own mother? But she wanted my help, and my Southern "gentlemanly" upbringing required that I respectfully grant aid requested by a lady—especially an elderly lady. So I escorted her to an unoccupied part of the auditorium, scrounged chairs for us, and sat patiently waiting for her to speak.

"I'm afraid God hasn't forgiven me."

That's all she said. Through her steady, incongruous smile, she continued to cry silently.

"God hasn't forgiven you of what?" I probed as gently as I knew how.

Hesitantly, she let scraps of her story escape, occasionally pausing to measure the judgment in my eyes before continuing. When she was a young, unmarried woman, she'd had sex with one of her boyfriends. That relationship ended, and she eventually found a Christian man with whom she'd formed a lifelong marriage. They'd worked side by side, raised godly children, been pillars in the church, and now lived in comfortable retirement. Comfortable except for one thing—she believed that when she died God would send her to hell for the sin of fornication.

"Have you told God how sorry you are for what you've done?" I asked.

"Thousands of times. For more than fifty years, I've begged Him to forgive me."

"You are a Christian, aren't you? I mean, you're not begging God to forgive you while refusing to trust in Jesus?"

"No. I became a Christian when I was a teenager. I just don't believe God has ever forgiven me for what I did."

"Have you told your husband about it? Maybe your guilt could be removed by knowing that nothing in your past is hidden from him."

"Yes, I told him. And he told me that he wasn't a virgin when we married either. I forgave him and he forgave me. I believe God has forgiven my husband. It's me who isn't forgiven."

She explained that she'd been taught that we will all someday stand before Christ and be judged for every action we've ever committed—good or bad—and that all of those acts will be revealed on that day to everyone present. She was filled with terror at the thought that her mother and her children would hear—or perhaps in some fashion even see—her sexual sin. I interrupted to ask what God meant when He said He puts our sins as far away from us as the east is from the west and when He said He'll remember our sins no more. She stared at me blankly. Those verses had no meaning for her. The God she'd been taught to serve intended to humiliate her with all her sins before all her friends on Judgment Day.

She had heard many sermons and Bible class lessons on the grace of God, but she had heard just as many—if not more—that heaped scathing judgments and used guilt to control and manipulate the gathered flock. The same preachers who cooed grace when they wanted to console, implemented a condemning theology when they felt the need to keep people on the straight and narrow.

She'd also been taught—chiefly through others' expectations—that the only way to make up for all the bad she'd done was to be obedient enough (read "good enough") to counterbalance her sin with her service to Christ. Of course, she couldn't do that. She could never be good enough to counterbalance a lifetime of evil thoughts, careless words, and sinful actions—even though she valiantly tried to do just that through a lifetime of devoted service to God and through the church. And if she couldn't balance out her adult life, how could she ever make up for the terrible sin of sleeping with her boyfriend when she was young? To her tortured conscience, that was her crowning sin, the proof of her inherent weakness, her ticket to hell.

She was in misery. Even if she could find some way to make up for her sin so she could be saved, God would still humiliate her before all mankind on Judgment Day.

When she finally fell silent, I growled in barely controlled rage, "They've lied to you!"

Oh, I wasn't angry with her. Never in my life have I felt more compassion, more desire to bind and heal. I was furious with the hordes of Satan who had kept this sister in guilt-bondage for more than half a century. Nor was my anger directed just at evil angels and demons. As much as anything, it was toward those humans who listen to demonic lies and who, by repeating those lies as the law of God, bring suffering into the lives of people like this spiritually depressed sister sitting beside me.

I don't need to tell you any more of her story except that it ended happily. But I mention her story at the outset of this book so I can ask you a question: Are you willing to examine *your* belief about forgiveness? Will you look honestly at the truth of God that sets us free?

If I had encountered only a few Christians during the last quarter-century who were burdened with a yoke of false guilt, I wouldn't think this matter so urgent. But again and again I see the disastrous effect of doctrines, taught by demons, that lead people to believe they have no access to the grace of God. These lies chain saints to false guilt.

I remember the lady at a workshop in Jackson, Tennessee, who said, "Thank you for preaching on the grace of God. This is the first time since I've become a Christian that I feel I may actually be saved!"

And on the Sunday before I wrote these words, a man visited our church as he passed through our city. He said, "I keep your tape series *Have Mercy* in my car and listen to it repeatedly. I have the tapes with me right now. They convince me of the grace of God and give me the strength to go on."

On the day I wrote this page, I received mail regarding a fine young preacher who tried to kill himself because of the guilt he feels for a sin he committed. Even though he teaches grace, he lives by guilt.

Yes, sin is serious! Yes, sin separates from God! But God's amazing grace offers relationship with Him, forgiveness forever, and life in Jesus. And that is what this book is about. By the grace of God, I want to share with you the grace of God!

You see, I understand grace from more than a theological framework. I am a sinner saved by grace.

You probably read my story at the beginning of this book.

Like King David, I've struggled with the overwhelming awareness of the consequences of my own behavior. My understanding of grace wasn't forged only through a study of the Word—even though the Word is the foundation. My own struggle with sin and my craving for forgiveness is what opened my eyes to truths of God—truths I could never have learned if I had not faced my weakness.

I need grace.

And I think you may be aware of your need for grace too.

Grace is not license to sin; it is freedom from guilt. Grace doesn't bring about perfection (the very concept of grace implies imperfection!), but it does bring purity. Grace creates a loyalty to God that leads to a godlier lifestyle than fear and dread ever could.

If you're wanting "forgiven forever" to mean that your sin is not all that bad, I pray God will speak to you about the seriousness of sin and the power of forgiveness.

If you think "forgiven forever" means you can continue in shameful sin, I pray God will convict your heart and bring you to repentance.

But if you hope "forgiven forever" is an avenue to peace and a basis for biblical hope, both in this life and the life to come, I pray God's message of forgiveness will take root in your heart and bring healing to your pain.

If this book leads you to a greater understanding of God's forgiveness, share what you learn with others. Perhaps you will want to gather people in a home Bible study or a class at church to study

God's forgiveness. I suggest you use the three-sermon video[1] that accompanies this book to begin the group and get the discussions started. Then, use this book to lead you through *the Book* to find the riches God has for you there.

I pray God's blessings on you as you discover the life-changing impact of God's forgiveness and embrace the full force of God's tender mercy.

PART ONE

UNDERSTANDING
GUILT

✣

Forgiveness is what takes place in God's heart. Healing is what happens in yours.

❧

For you who revere my name, the sun of righteousness will rise with healing in its wings. And you will go out and leap like calves released from the stall.

Malachi 4:2

What Good Is Guilt?

Tanned, young, and smartly dressed—from his fashionably placed earrings to his perfectly casual loafers—Rick looked as if he had stepped smoothly from the pages of *GQ*. He was the type of man women sneaked second glances at and men felt threatened by . . . unless they were casting their own second glances. As he came nearer, weaving his way through the throng, I found myself thinking that those lusting after or envying him on this night would feel their passion falter as quickly as they found his tormented eyes.

His eyes carried death.

I'd known Rick years before when I'd tried unsuccessfully to help him. As he reached me, he nodded his head in greeting, seemingly oblivious to the people filing past us into the rapidly filling church auditorium. When he spoke, it was without the preamble of niceties or homage paid to old times.

"I'm dying, Joe."

I didn't say anything because I didn't know what to say. I immediately knew what he was dying from, yet it didn't seem possible that this apparently healthy man could have *that* disease. He understood my silence—he'd already experienced it from his parents when he told them. He continued, now speaking barely above a whisper in deference to passersby.

"I have AIDS and I'm scared. There's nothing anybody can do to change the fact that I'm going to die a horrible death." He paused to wipe at the mist bathing his eyes. "I don't want to die like this. Can you help me?"

Of course I would help. I loved him. I hadn't known how to help him when I was younger, but I could help him now. I spoke carefully, my eyes locked on his in an effort to read every nuance of his reaction to what I was about to say. "Yes, Rick, I'll help. I believe God works powerfully, and I believe in God's mercy and grace. I'll get the elders of this church, and we'll pray fervently that God will heal you and . . ."

"No! That's not what I'm asking! I'm not afraid of death. In some ways I find it desirable—a way out of the mess I've made of my life. I don't want God to heal my body. I want Him to heal me! I'm scared of Him, and I can't stand the thought of facing Him with what I've done and what I am.

"Joe, forgive me if my language offends you, but I've been a slut. There's just no other way to put it. My homosexual desires got stronger over the years, in spite of what counselor after counselor did to try to help me. I worked for an escort service. I hung out in bars and went home with people I didn't know to do things you don't want to hear. I've been thrown out of places. I've been beaten. Oh, Joe, you can never understand the humiliation and terror of being beaten mercilessly—fists, filthy names, and hatred coming at me nonstop—because someone found out I was 'gay.'

"The reason I can't stand the idea of facing God with this is because all the time I knew better! You tried to help me. Other people tried to help me. My parents begged and prayed and cried.

Don't you understand? I will have absolutely no excuse when I stand before God. He's going to humiliate me and punish me more than those homophobes ever did!"

Once or twice during his soliloquy I tried to interrupt, to interject a kind word or a calming thought, but Rick wouldn't let me. His fear and hatred for himself propelled him like an out-of-control bulldozer. The only thing to do was get out of his way until he ran out of fuel. Finally, slowly, he lurched to a halt.

"Rick, have you asked God to forgive you?" The question wasn't as unkind as it sounds. I just needed information, quickly, before he restarted his self-flagellation.

His body sagged and his head dropped as he replied so quietly that I had to lean forward to hear. "That's the mysterious part of all this. I gave myself totally to God a couple of months ago—body and soul. And I've actually enjoyed living the way my mom taught me from the Bible when I was a kid. I go to church. I pray. I read my Bible. I'm living a good life." His agitation sputtered back to life, and he started to cry. "But I still have this dread of meeting God."

"Rick, I understand how you feel. More than that, I believe I understand the problem that causes this dread you feel. By the grace of God, Rick, I believe I also have found God's solution. I wasn't talking about the elders praying just for your physical healing, though I do want to pray for that. What I most want them to pray for is your spiritual healing. God can get you past this fear of facing Him. It won't happen overnight, but with time and a better understanding of God's grace, God can heal your heart. There is a difference between being *forgiven* of a sin and being *healed* of a sin. Forgiveness is what takes place in God's heart. Healing is what happens in yours."

25

As Rick learned the power of that truth, his healing began to happen. It didn't come overnight, but today he carries absolutely no dread of God.

Perhaps you relate to Rick's story—I know I do. I know what it is to believe God has forgiven me yet still feel the weight of guilt. I understand what it means to be theologically forgiven but emotionally tormented. Maybe you do too. It makes little difference whether your sin is homosexual prostitution, adultery, murder, stealing, greed, or lying. Whatever it is that you've done, or are still doing, God wants not only to *forgive* you, He wants to *heal* you.

He said so.

To the sinful people of Isaiah's day, God gave a message of healing and hope.

> I live in a high and holy place, but also with him who is contrite and lowly in spirit, to revive the spirit of the lowly and to revive the heart of the contrite. . . . I have seen his ways, but I will heal him; I will guide him and restore comfort to him, creating praise on the lips of the mourners in Israel. Peace, peace, to those far and near. . . . I will heal them.[1]

The God of heaven, in spite of what He has seen you do, offers you revival, comfort, peace, direction . . . and healing.

Two Extreme Views of Grace and Guilt

Being healed of sin may not make sense to those who've never suffered inordinate grief over their sins. It seems that as I travel the world speaking for churches, I meet people with two extreme views of grace and guilt—those who use grace as a license to sin and therefore seldom, if ever, feel guilt and those who can't believe grace is for them and are therefore debilitated by guilt.

Those in the first group I call *spiritual sociopaths.* For them, grace carries only theological meaning because, in their view, guilt exists only intellectually. Those in the second group—*spiritual cripples*—see God's mercy and grace as unattainable and abstract, a gift from God for others but not for themselves.

It is to you in that second group that I write a message of hope. God has the power to take away your sin, to remove your guilt, and to heal you of the self-degradation and spiritual doubt that torment you.

But before we explore Satan's strategies to cripple, we must first have some understanding of those who feel no guilt at all.

Spiritual Sociopaths

Some people act as if they have a license to sin. They believe that God's mercy and grace will forgive them of anything, so that's exactly what they do—anything—with few or no twinges of conscience.

One sister in Christ told me she was leaving her husband to marry the lover with whom she'd been having a torrid affair for more than a year. I pointedly asked her how she could justify being sexually involved with this man when God made it clear how He felt: "Marriage should be honored by all, and the marriage bed kept pure, for God will judge the adulterer and all the sexually immoral."[2] She blithely replied that God didn't mind her relationship with her lover, for He had sent the lover to her in the first place!

During the spring of 1995, I channel-surfed into *Friends,* the number-one program on television at the time, to find Representative Newt Gingrich's sister portraying a minister performing a lesbian wedding. Open Bible in hand, she proclaimed to millions of viewers that God is love and that He honors all loving unions, even homosexual marriages.

I don't know how to convict people of sin when they convince themselves that God partners in their sinfulness.

Those who think God's grace gives total license, and therefore feel no guilt, have their own spiritual problems—serious spiritual problems. Jesus called them hypocrites. The difference between hypocrites and sinners is that sinners admit they sin. Hypocrites refuse to feel guilt for their actions. Jesus clearly stated what He thinks of that: "Hypocrites . . . are like whitewashed tombs, which look beautiful on the outside but on the inside are full of dead men's bones and everything unclean . . . on the outside [they] appear to people as righteous but on the inside [they] are full of hypocrisy and wickedness."[3] This extreme, hypocritical view of grace can eventually lead one to become a *spiritual sociopath*.

Psychological sociopaths know no feelings of guilt or remorse. Psychological sociopaths steal, lie, or kill without any thought for their victims. If they ever assign blame for their actions, it always falls to someone else. Nothing bad they do is ever their fault, and everything bad that happens to them is the fault of someone else.

Russ Jurek, the family minister at the church where I am a member, displays a cartoon in his office that shows a therapist sitting next to a patient reclining on a couch. The counselor is saying, "We can save time by using the device on the wall," and he's pointing to a wheel for the patient to spin. The place the arrow stops indicates the person responsible for the patient's problem. Broad areas offer possibilities like *society*, *mother*, and *father*. A very narrow option is labeled *myself*.

We chuckle at how the cartoon pokes fun at the lack of personal responsibility some people feel for the problems in their lives. Yet that's how sociopaths operate.

Now, take that psychological concept and apply it to spiritual behavior. A spiritual sociopath feels no guilt or remorse before God. Like psychological sociopaths, spiritual sociopaths sin willingly with no concern for the victims of their sins. All they consider is their own personal advantage. They are like the people Peter described when he wrote: "With eyes full of adultery, they never stop sinning; they seduce the unstable; they are experts in greed—an accursed brood!"[4]

People who feel no guilt are spiritual sociopaths.

Strong statement isn't it? If you are confused about your spiritual identity, it may cause you to feel anxious. But it is unlikely you are a spiritual sociopath. While you may occasionally act like one, that doesn't necessarily mean you are. Thousands upon thousands of Christians, at some point, cycle through periods where they sin, ignoring the consequences for others and not allowing themselves to feel guilt. For a period of time they live as people deceived, and if a snapshot were taken of that section of their lives, they may well be diagnosed as spiritual sociopaths. But there is a major difference between struggling Christians temporarily deceived and people who never feel guilt and never concern themselves with the effects of their acts on others.

We understand the difference between someone doing an evil act and being a sociopath in the psychological world. Recently I watched with fascinated revulsion a television news program in which a reporter interviewed convicted teenage murderers. Without exception, each had done a terrible act of mayhem on one or more fellow human beings. But as each in turn came on the screen, he showed remorse for his evil deed and shamefully lamented his actions. While each young man phrased it somewhat differently, they all said something like, "I can't believe I did it. When I try to remember it, parts are missing, and the parts I can remember are vague and dreamlike. I don't know how I could have done such a terrible thing."

At least some, if not all, of those boys told the truth as they described their contrition. They spoke of unspeakable deeds but they didn't speak as unaffected sociopaths. They cared and they cried. They would have undone their actions if they could. Sinners yes. Sociopaths no.

The same is true of many Christians who commit sins that shatter their lives or the lives of people they love. One man who had been an active leader in his church tried to explain his embezzling company funds to me. "I've had a lot of time to try to figure out how I could have done such an awful thing. Oh, no, I don't try to justify myself. Who could possibly justify what I did to my family and to my church? I could tell you about the struggle in my marriage over a continual lack of money, about the years of deteriorating relationship with my wife, and the rage I felt that I couldn't seem to get my finances under control. Explaining all that might help you understand, but it wouldn't justify. Whether you understand or not, that sense of hopelessness finally brought me to sin's door. I felt as if my life was going to be miserable for as long as I lived.

"I remember the day it happened. Everything's like a dream to me now. Some parts of it gone altogether. The overwhelming guilt I felt as I juggled books, altered receipts, stole the money.

"Joe, it was the worst thing I've ever done, but surely that doesn't mean that I'm inherently evil, does it? I care. I hurt for all those I hurt. And for myself. I would do anything if I could just get that day back and live it over."

If you struggle with guilt over some act in your life, you may feel just like this Christian man. The act you feel so badly about was probably a very bad thing to do. Something you shouldn't have done. But don't think that evil act, no matter how bad it was, necessarily means you are a spiritual sociopath.

Sociopaths don't seek the healing of God.

The simple fact that you are reading this book indicates that you are looking for spiritual healing—either for yourself or for the people to whom you minister. Your pain or your desire proves you are not a spiritual sociopath. While you need to be aware of that extreme, you don't need to worry about it.

Now let's move on to the second extreme view of grace and guilt—the one on which this book focuses.

Spiritual Cripples

People who are crippled by guilt worry me just as much as those who use grace for license. These Christians have little or no sense of salvation. They committed themselves to Christ earlier in their lives and try to obey Him, yet they walk in constant fear that they have angered God or somehow inadvertently "fallen from grace." The only time they know spiritual comfort is when they work themselves into exhaustion doing Christian deeds. Then, as the fatigue fades, guilt and doubt return, sinking them slowly into a swamp of spiritual quicksand that smothers the breath of God within them.

I meet these guilt-caged Christians everywhere.

Recently a young minister spent hours with me reciting his wickedness, describing it graphically so I would fully appreciate the enormity of his evil. He needed another Christian to agree that his sin existed in monstrous proportions. No matter how much he prayed, studied, praised, or worked, his guilt subsided not a whit. While he knew exactly which Scriptures to teach others so they could allow God to remove their guilt, he couldn't apply those powerful passages of comfort and hope to himself.

Guilt-trapped Christians never can.

While this young minister never perpetrated the same sins as Rick, he endured the same spiritual attack and suffered the same spiritual sickness. The sickness that leads to becoming a spiritual cripple.

If Satan cannot deceive you into becoming a spiritual sociopath, he tries to make you a spiritual cripple. Living up to his nature,[5] he and his well-trained, silver-tongued, battle-sophisticated hordes of demons, evil angels, and sin-controlled people know just how to convince you that even God doesn't love a hypocritical sinner like you.

Unless you overcome their deceptive tactics, Satan's forces may succeed in crippling you by one of their attacks.

Satan Reminds You of Your Past

Satan and his cohorts try to deceive you into believing you're a hypocrite by tempting you to relive fantasies of enthralling sins from your past. They attempt to convince you that you're evil to the core by showing you that you still desire things that offend God. What they neglect to tell you is that almost everyone who ever sinned has experienced the same afterlust. But afterlust shows the power of the temptation, not residual evil in the sinner.

At Family Dynamics, we work with many couples whose marriages were brought to the edge of destruction for one reason or another. As you would imagine, some of those jeopardized marriages got that way because one or both mates became involved with another person. When I first started working with couples in this situation, seeing genuine penitence, watching them beg for forgiveness and another chance, I would have guessed that the straying partner would never be tempted to involvement with the lover again. It didn't take long to learn how naive I was.

No, I don't mean to imply that these folks want to go back to the lover or to the sin. They want to work things out with their mates and have a wonderful, happy marriage. But any sinner will on occasion find himself mentally reliving the aspects of the sin that first attracted them. A song on the radio, passing a certain restaurant, or seeing someone in the mall who at first glance appears to be the abandoned lover. Any of these or a hundred other things immediately propel the person to a mental place he doesn't want to be.

Does that mean a lack of genuine penitence? A lack of spirituality? A core of evil within?

No. Like it or not, it proves only that we are human.

Having experienced some afterlust myself, I'm thrilled that God doesn't expect us to become divine—or even superhuman—in order to receive His loving, healing grace. He gives it to humans with human weaknesses. So when Satan's forces try to deceive with that ploy, all us forgiven Christians can say, "Sorry. I may still be human. But I'm also still forgiven!"

Satan Attacks You through Fellow Christians

Sometimes Satan tries to make you question your integrity by attacking you with the words of Christians whom he manipulates into maligning your character and motives. He knows that brothers attacking brothers is a strong ploy toward making a believer spiritually despondent. Even the strongest Christians may question their relationship with God when other Christians condemn them.

It's no mistake on God's part to show us in the book of Job that His humble servant could stand most anything until he received the attack of misguided brothers. Job endured the death of his children, the loss of his fortune, and severe pain and suffering in acute disease. He even overcame the weakness of a distraught wife. Only when the brothers attacked his integrity did he waver. Only then did he foolishly demand God get Himself down here to explain.

God told us that story so we would know that the Devil will always attack His people through that proven method. Centuries before we were born, He answered our questions and quieted our doubts that would arise from such attacks. He lets us know where the attacks originate (Satan) and how to endure them (trust).

Satan Confuses You through Self-Appointed Counselors

Occasionally Satan tries to confuse you through supposed insight shared by self-important (and often self-appointed) counselors who claim to know more about your "inmost being" than you do—even though God flatly states that this is impossible.[6] That's what happened to Rick. The counselor he saw regularly told him he was lying to himself about his desire to quit sinning and obey God. The counselor, steeped in her own sense of what brokenness is, refused to accept Rick's sorrow and turmoil as signs of penitence. She told him he would never find the forgiveness of God and peace in his heart until he truly yielded to God. When he asked her how he would know he had done that, she replied that he would know when she told him he had. Rick asked me, "Can she really know something about me that I'm afraid to admit to myself? Is she right that I haven't yielded to God even though I've thrown myself at His feet begging for mercy?"

I told him, "Rick, sometimes we lie to ourselves and others see the lie in us. But that isn't true here. No Christian has the right to tell you that your broken, contrite actions aren't good enough, that you aren't yet penitent enough to be forgiven. Your counselor is trying to make you meet her criteria for healing, not God's. She cannot know your heart. Only you and God can know your heart."[7]

Satan Reinterprets God's Good News

Perhaps the forces of evil have tried to misdirect you by reinterpreting God's truth. Instead of hearing the good news of God's love taught by loving, compassionate teachers, you hear only His wrath. And so instead of running to Him for deliverance, you flee from Him in terror.

I've hopelessly watched it happen. Seen people go out a side door rather than let me talk with them. Or leave the revival sermon, head hung low and spirit broken. When others in the audience heard God's condemnation of sin coupled with His loving grace that will remove it, these people heard only the condemnation. It's as if satanic forces blinded them, temporarily deafened them, and locked them onto one phrase or scripture so they couldn't see anything else that happened.

What more evil could they do than pervert the good news of Jesus with a message of hopelessness.

Sometimes evil forces go even further and use preachers, teachers, or authors to actually pervert the good news of life into dismal news of death. Paul said of such men and women who allow themselves to be used like that:

> The Spirit clearly says that in later times some will abandon the faith and follow deceiving spirits and things taught by demons. Such teachings come through hypocritical liars, whose consciences have been seared as with a hot iron. They forbid people to marry and order them to abstain from certain foods, which God created to be received with thanksgiving by those who believe and who know the truth. For everything God created is good, and nothing is to be rejected if it is received with thanksgiving.[8]

Notice Paul's reference to how demonic teaching forbids marriage. I've seen people whose marriages were destroyed by such teaching given through hypocritical church leaders. One woman divorced her Christian husband at the encouragement of her church after leaders told her he was a reprobate because he refused to accept some of their exclusionary teachings. They convinced her

35

she would stand guilty before God if she didn't end the marriage. They taught her nothing of grace and love, only isolation and enmity.[9] Another man refused his wife sexual fulfillment because his church told him he was committing adultery by having sex with his own wife! They convinced him that he had no right to be married to her and would certainly go to hell if he ever touched her in any sexual way. They never offered grace or forgiveness, only a lifetime of frustration and anger.[10] In both cases, Satan used church people to make spiritual cripples of God's children.

The forces of Satan never play fair, but they always play hard. They'll do anything to make you believe God has not and never will forgive you for what you've done and who you are. They'll manipulate you into negative emotions of guilt, rage, and frustration for as long as they can—a lifetime, if possible.

Lies.

All lies.

But very effective lies to many people.

People who believe these lies about themselves become terrified (like Rick) or cynical about themselves (like the minister who wanted me to agree with him about his total wickedness) or isolated and lonely (like the man who refused to enjoy the blessings of marriage with his spouse). For them, prayer ceases. The Bible morphs from words of life into words of discouragement and death. The fruit of the Spirit dissipates, and the works of the flesh quietly resume their control of the demoralized Christian.

NEITHER EXTREME IS OF GOD

Of course, neither of the two extreme views of grace and guilt —neither spiritual sociopath nor spiritual cripple—are correct. God wants us to enjoy our salvation. We have every right to rejoice in the confidence of our relationship with God through our Lord

Jesus and the indwelling Holy Spirit. But that true enjoyment never leads to a disregard of evil. As Paul said at the end of his wonderful exposition on grace, "What shall we say, then? Shall we go on sinning so that grace may increase? By no means! We died to sin; how can we live in it any longer?"[11]

No, God doesn't want us to feel we have license to sin. But neither does He want us to be crippled by fear—believing that we've lost our relationship with Him. He wants us to know when we've sinned. He even wants us to feel and mourn our sin. But He doesn't want His children to fear Him or live in dread of meeting Him in death. He wants us to feel His forgiveness.

Christians who don't admit their sins and who never feel guilt for them don't understand *God*. Christians who live with constant guilt because of their sins don't understand *grace*. Christians who receive God's healing understand both.

They also understand guilt.

God's purpose for guilt lies between the two extremes. He wants us to feel guilt and be motivated by it to act, but He doesn't want us debilitated by it.

As we've already seen, if we had no capacity to feel guilt, we would be in dire spiritual jeopardy. The ability to experience guilt is essential to our spiritual health. In fact, guilt does in the spiritual realm what pain does in the physical realm.

THE POSITIVE POWER OF PAIN AND GUILT

Normal people don't like pain. We avoid it whenever possible, and we keep our medicine cabinets full of ointments, pills, and remedies to eliminate it as quickly as it appears. But even with our dislike for pain, we know how essential it is to our physical well-being.

Richard Rogers of Lubbock, Texas, tells of seeing lepers in Third World countries who have no fingers or toes. Because their disease destroys their bodies' ability to feel pain, these poor lepers, forced to sleep in the streets or wilderness, have no awareness when rodents feed on them in the stillness of the night. Without pain, their bodies have no warning signal shrieking, "Stop! Something's wrong! Fix it now!" They sleep through the nocturnal attacks and awaken to discover the horrible assault the next morning.

Even a baby's pain, though unsettling to parents, must exist for the child to survive. When our firstborn, Angel, cried incessantly, a bright, young pediatrician doggedly tracked her pain and low-grade fever until he discovered the hidden cause. Without her pain, we wouldn't have known that something of life-threatening consequence was wrong. Without pain, she would have died.

God designed physical pain to warn of damage or disease and to compel us to seek physical health.

That means physical pain is good.

But it can also be bad.

Unceasing pain works against us rather than for us. If, for example, a person has an injury or disease that creates unending, unmanageable pain, the sufferer becomes physically debilitated. The pain no longer serves its original purpose of compelling the person to seek physical health, because the possibility of physical health no longer exists. The pain God meant to help becomes a tool of Satan to incapacitate.

In a similar way, God designed personal guilt to warn of spiritual damage or disease so that we are compelled to seek spiritual health. Just as physical pain operates on our physical senses, spiritual pain—guilt—operates on our spiritual senses. When we stray spiritually from the way of God, guilt causes our spirits within us to scream, "Stop! Something's wrong! Fix it now!"

I can give you an excellent example.

Back in the 1960s, Marshall Underwood was the most gifted high-school quarterback to play football in Foley, Alabama, since the famed Kenny Stabler who went on to NFL fame. Marshall broke record after record set by Stabler at that high school. Naturally, the best colleges, including powerhouse football universities in the Southeastern Conference, tried to recruit him to play for their teams. He decided on Auburn University and had a stellar freshman year there. The confident predictions in the state of Alabama were that he would experience an unbelievable college football career and then take his turn as a famous quarterback in the NFL. His fame and fortune were set.

I met Marshall Underwood in his sophomore year of college—not at Auburn University—but at a small Bible college, then named Alabama Christian College, now Faulkner University. He was there as a Bible major. He'd given up football forever.

Of course, I and all my classmates had to know why. How could he walk away from all that every high-school player in the state craved? Had he been hurt? Did college ball prove his ability to be overrated? What happened?

It was guilt.

Marshall said that the things he did as a freshman football hero and the things he watched other idolized athletes do brought him to the conviction that he didn't have the spiritual stamina to serve God and live in that world. He was so spiritually pained that he walked away from sure fame and fortune and pursued a Bible degree so he could become a minister. To this day Marshall Underwood ministers for a church in Mobile, Alabama—the same church he's ministered to since he left college.

I can also tell you that to this day I respect Marshall as one of the most godly men I've ever known.

Over the years, we've talked many times about his abandoning football. Once, wistfully, with his eyes focused on something I couldn't see, he shared, "Sometimes in the fall when I hear those marching-band drums, I feel a great sense of loss. I feel this strong desire to be on that field throwing those precise pass patterns and hearing thousands of fans cheering, marshaling my team to victory." I sat quietly as he drifted and dreamed in that world. Finally, he refocused on me. "Sometimes people tell me they believe I could have made it in football and been the Christian I should be. But I don't think so. At that age and with those temptations, I wouldn't have survived. And by choosing this route, God has allowed me to be a vital part of the lives of many. I miss football, but I made the right choice. I'm glad God sent me on this path instead."

Marshall changed his course in life and became a powerful tool for God's kingdom because of the personal guilt he felt about his lifestyle as a football hero. That's guilt doing what God meant it to do.

You, too, have probably experienced times in your spiritual life when guilt shouted at you to stop some course you had set and delivered you from greater spiritual pain.

That's why guilt is good.

People who cannot experience physical pain live in danger of disfigurement and death. Those who cannot experience spiritual pain live in danger of encroaching sin and spiritual destruction. So, is guilt always a tool of God?

No.

Unfortunately, Satan counterfeits every wonderful thing of God, including guilt. God created love; Satan counterfeited love with lust. God gives magnificent abilities; Satan counterfeits them with pride or arrogance. How does Satan counterfeit guilt? He does it by heaping unrelenting personally felt guilt on people whom God has already forgiven. It's that unrelenting guilt that makes spiritual cripples.

So, does God want us to feel guilty? Yes. God wants us to feel guilt in our hearts when we sin. He doesn't want us to be hypocrites or spiritual sociopaths. God made guilt to warn us: "Something is wrong! Fix it!"

He wants your personal guilt to motivate you to seek Him for healing. But he doesn't want Satan's forces to use guilt to cripple us—and they will try.

Every sin is strongly condemned, but every sinner is loved unconditionally.

You see, if you're a Christian, the forces of Satan can't steal your salvation, but they can steal your joy. And, sadly, there is the possibility that they can convince you to walk away from all the blessings God offers you.

Good news: We're going to put guilt in the proper perspective. God's healing is here.

It's time you accept His mercy.

It's time you accept His forgiveness.

It's time to let God heal you.

While we are legally guilty the
very moment we sin, we do not
experience personal guilt until we
admit to ourselves and before
God the utter wrongfulness of
the act.

꿈

Let us draw near to God with a sincere
heart in full assurance of faith, having our
hearts sprinkled to cleanse us from a guilty
conscience and having our bodies washed
with pure water.

Hebrews 10:22

2

Where Does Guilt Come From?

Not an object in his office had the grit to move a millimeter out of place—each fully aware of the immediate consequence of such reckless audacity. As I scanned the room, I wondered what madness led the paper clips to jumble carelessly in their clear plastic container and entertained the fleeting thought that they would surely come to order the moment Lawrence looked their direction. I'd met many detailed, analytical people, but Lawrence operated at world-class level. It was almost incomprehensible that he, of all people, could have made such a mess of his life. And now he wanted me, of all people, to precisely answer the question that he felt would give him the key to recovery.

A few years earlier Lawrence had fallen in love with a client and, contrary to his life-pattern, allowed intense emotion to whisk him out of his twenty-five year marriage into an affair and subsequent marriage to his lover. The new union didn't last "happily ever after." Guilt eroded the relationship with his new wife, his church excommunicated him, and his children shut him out of their lives.

Lawrence's life crumbled around him. In great pain, he realized he'd lost nearly everything important to him.

In the third year of this second marriage, Lawrence initiated divorce proceedings. He shut himself away from everyone except business associates and sent for help.

I, of course, was the help.

As Lawrence concluded a brief but thorough recap of his situation, he told me what he needed. "I feel tremendous guilt, and it's killing me. What I want to know is, why didn't I feel guilt when I had the affair? Why didn't I feel it when my wife and children tried to get me to drop the divorce? Why does guilt steadily plague me now, when back then I didn't feel it at all?" He paused to make sure I was hearing every word, then he made his point. "If I had felt then what I feel now, I never would have done what I did. If I could just understand how that happened to me, maybe I could get some handle on how I got to where I am. Don't give me any psychology; I've got a therapist for that. I want to know if the Bible speaks to this. Just explain *where* guilt comes from and *when* it comes."

In his analytical way, Lawrence started just where he should have. Sometimes the cure for physical ailment shouldn't be administered until the sufferer understands the cause and nature of the disease. Not only does that understanding ensure the implementation of the correct cure, it also helps the patient avoid contracting the disease again. That principle can have just as much application in the spiritual world as it does in the medical world.

I can relate to Lawrence's dilemma, and maybe you can as well. The guilt I felt came far too late to deter my spiritual delusion. My sin also brought intensely destructive consequences to my life. During the sin and shortly thereafter, I experienced more of a spiritual numbness than anything of positive spiritual value. But no one can stay numb forever, and slowly guilt began to grow in me until I found it difficult to live with myself. In the dark hours before dawn, I often lay awake wishing I could go back in time, face the situation again, and this time handle it without the sin.

Does any of that sound familiar to you? If so, you may have contemplated the same questions Lawrence and I asked. If guilt is such a strong motivator to repent, why isn't it just as strong a motivator to stop a sensitive Christian from sinning?

The answer to this question lies in understanding the two kinds of guilt—*legal* and *personal*. Legal guilt exists before God, and personal guilt exists within an individual. The difference between the two is crucial.

To understand guilt—and to find God's healing for it—you must first understand how God views sin and guilt. Guilt isn't just psychological or emotional. It exists not only within you, but also before God. God views your guilt as a reality that must be dealt with so that He may be appeased. In order for you to overcome personal guilt, you must first overcome legal guilt. God cannot heal your heart until you let Him remove your sin. And you will not understand that removal until you accept the reality of the sin in your life.

LEGAL GUILT

Let's look at how Scripture explains legal guilt. If you read Leviticus chapters 4 through 7, you will notice that as God gives the law through Moses, He lists offerings that are to be given, such as the burnt offering, grain offering, sin offering, and fellowship offering. Included in that list is the guilt offering. This offering gives us great insight into God's view of sin and guilt. He shows us that He considers guilt a thing with substance and reality. It isn't a concept; it's an actual entity. More than that, God reveals to us three broad categories of sin that result in legal guilt: *unintentional* sin, *ignorant* sin, and *willful* sin.

Unintentional Sin

In Leviticus 5:14–16, Moses refers to unintentional violation of the law. Although the person knows he or she committed the sin, it wasn't premeditated. There was no intent.

There were two general ways in which people could sin unintentionally under the Law of Moses: One was by what they *did,* and the other was by what they *didn't* do. Moses describes the first as when a person "does what is forbidden in any of the Lord's commands."[1] He describes the second this way: "When a person commits a violation and sins unintentionally in regard to any of the Lord's holy things . . . he must make restitution for what he has failed to do in regard to the holy things."[2]

You're probably familiar with unintentional sins. If you've ever pounded your thumb with a self-willed hammer and instantly reacted by bellowing uncivilized words that sent your children scurrying for safety, you know what it is to commit an unintentional sin. Perhaps you thought nothing of it, but if those words were profane, you sinned and created guilt before God.[3]

Or perhaps you began dressing smarter, smelling better, and walking lighter because of a new person at work. Maybe, as you cuddled your mate on the sofa, you found yourself daydreaming about holding that person instead. If so, you know something about unintentional sin. You didn't mean to become enamored with someone other than your spouse. While you took some comfort in knowing you didn't intend it and weren't seeking it, you finally had to admit that your attraction had reached the point of being sinful.[4] God, however, had already taken note of the sin.

Before the standard of the law of God, it makes no difference that a person didn't intend to commit a sin. Intentional or not, sin violates God's will. God tells us in these verses in Leviticus that every sin carries with it the element He calls *guilt*.

Even unintentional sins.

Ignorant Sin

Because God's law stands as absolute authority, He imposes it on His people in everything they do, even the things they aren't aware of. "If a person sins and does what is forbidden in any of the Lord's commands, even though he does not know it, he is guilty and will be held responsible. . . . He has been guilty of wrongdoing against the Lord."[5]

You may be wondering, "How can I sin before God and not know I've sinned?" It can happen in many ways. A Christian still learning the Word of God may violate God's will without knowing the action is sinful. As I've grown in my relationship with Jesus over the years, I've discovered truths that were there all along but were somehow veiled to me. Apparently that happens to others as well. I heard one preacher say, "Sometimes I'm reading through my Bible and I stumble on a plain, simple truth that I've never seen before. My first reaction is, 'When did that get in there?' "

As Christians learn new truths, we change our actions immediately. But even quitting a sinful action immediately doesn't change the fact that we already violated God's will. God makes it clear that ignorance doesn't affect the sinfulness of the act.

Absolute law demands absolute obedience.

Without excuse.

Perhaps you're thinking, "I don't buy it. Surely God doesn't hold people responsible for sins they don't even know they do!" Well, if the verse cited above doesn't convince you, maybe an illustration will help: Imagine you borrow your brother-in-law's car because yours is in the repair shop. He doesn't remember to tell you that when he replaced his worn-out tires with new tires of a different size, it caused the speedometer reading to be five miles slow. Thus, when it reads fifty-five, the car is really going sixty. In your ignorance, you blissfully drive through a fifty-five mile-per-hour speed zone at a cool sixty, and a state trooper pulls you over for being five miles an hour over the speed limit. Will either he or the judge consider you innocent because you didn't know you were speeding? Absolutely not. As far as the law is concerned, you're guilty. The trooper has the right to write the ticket, and the judge has the right to levy the fine, no matter how much you plead that you didn't know you were speeding. The judge can demand the money without blinking an eye. As a matter of fact, you may notice that the judge's only hint of emotion is a slight lip curl and a smug intonation, "Ignorance is no excuse."

Believe me, I know.

It happened in 1983, and I remember it as if it were yesterday.

You may find yourself thinking, "But that's not how God operates!" Yes, it is. God says that sin is the transgression of the law.[6] He didn't say that sin is when you *know* you transgress the law. Sin happens whenever you break God's law.

Several years ago in an adult Bible lesson I taught, I examined sins found in the Bible that were more clearly explained in the Old Testament. A day or so after our class session, a young Christian woman from the class asked for an appointment. With great embarrassment, she confessed her involvement in one of those sins. Hoping I wouldn't think her evil, she said, "I had no idea that what I did was wrong. I'd never seen or heard that verse before we read it in class together, and I've been going to church for twenty-six years. I just didn't know."

I understood her predicament, and I felt great compassion for the guilt she felt. But I also knew she had violated God's law.

I think the apostle Paul may have related to her situation. When he served God as a Pharisee, he served Him with complete sincerity, convinced he was obeying God. Unfortunately for the church, his misunderstanding caused great misery. As Paul headed to Damascus, "breathing out murderous threats against the Lord's disciples,"[7] he did it with a clear conscience and pure heart.[8] Ignorantly, he thought his actions served God, when in truth they served Satan.

Even though his clear conscience followed him into Christianity, he understood that it never justified his sin. He was guided by the Holy Spirit to write, "My conscience is clear, but that does not make me innocent. It is the Lord who judges me."[9]

Obviously, ignorant sins don't cause feelings of personal guilt. How could they when we don't know we've done something wrong? God's point is clear: Guilt isn't just what we feel. Guilt stands as a reality before Him.

Just about now you may find yourself thinking, "Whoa! I'm reading the wrong book! I'm looking for healing from guilt and here you are telling me I may be guilty of things I don't even know about!"

Don't panic. This is a book about healing, forgiveness, and godly peace. But the only way to fully appreciate and completely accept God's grace and mercy is to understand His view of sin and His displeasure with it. I'm convinced that people who downplay sin do a tremendous injustice to themselves and those they try to help. Sin always creates guilt before God.

Now let's look at the third type of sin that causes legal guilt, the one that usually produces the strongest personal guilt.

Willful Sin

After listing guilt offerings for unintentional sin and ignorant sin, God discusses willful sin—sin we know better than to do but do anyway.[10] Both unintentional and ignorant sins share a lack of intent to disobey God. That's why they're usually easier to deal with. While sensitive Christians deplore any sin, unintentional or ignorant sins seem to affect most of us with much less impact than intentional sins. We feel bad about them, but not too bad. After all, we didn't mean to disobey and surely that should count for something.

But intentional sins are quite different creatures. We have no excuse unless we boldly lie to ourselves. And even the best "self-liar" can barely contain the personal guilt feelings born of intentional sin.

David called intentional sins "willful sins" in Psalm 19:13. The word translated as "willful" in the New International Version and "presumptuous" in the King James Version and New American Standard Bible is from the Hebrew word *zed*. It means arrogant, proud, presumptuous, or insolent. That's just what intentional sins are. When you know God says something is wrong but you do it anyway, you are being arrogant and insolent.

I see it often in people I try to help. I vividly remember encountering it as I counseled a minister and the woman from his church with whom he'd committed adultery. They described vividly the confusion of hating the sin, loving the affair, and rebelling against God while longing for Him. At the outset, their guilt drove them to their knees in prayer each time they consummated their rendezvous. They begged God to forgive them. They asked Him to help them stop sinning with each other. They cried, embraced, pledged eternal love, and departed with conflicting cravings for forgiveness and for each other. Within a week they would lose their spiritual struggle and meet again to repeat the drama with little change in script or direction. With time, they quit praying. Instead they ended each engagement planning where and when they would next meet.

I knew this minister well. He preached the Bible truthfully and courageously. Both he and his paramour could quickly guide anyone to Scriptures condemning adultery. They knew that their sin drifted as a decaying stench before God. They knew that if His voice spoke directly to them as they caressed and consoled each other, it would thunder, "You who say that people should not commit adultery, do you commit adultery?"[11]

That's willful sin.

Arrogant sin.

Insolent sin.

Even their struggle, shame, and sorrow could not alter the fact that their forbidden sexual union comprised an act of sheer arrogance before God. No matter what the circumstance, it is presumptuous sin when we disobey God in any matter—even matters we think are small or inconsequential—when we clearly know what He expects from us.

Legal guilt comes from violating God—unintentionally, ignorantly, or willingly. Personal guilt comes from an inner, convicting realization that we have offended the God of heaven and that we have failed to live up to what we believe and want to be.

PERSONAL GUILT

While we are legally guilty the very moment we sin, we do not experience personal guilt until we admit to ourselves the utter wrongfulness of the act. As long as we continue to violate God's law, our mounting guilt is a legal reality, but it isn't a personal reality. Until we acknowledge our sin, our guilt builds in our spirits and in the annals of heaven but not in our hearts.

At least not yet.

When something finally penetrates our veils, personal guilt drifts over us and we *feel* guilty. Personal guilt touches the emotions and evokes negative feelings like *doubt, fear,* and *shame.* People who feel guilty typically *doubt* their relationship with God and their ability to overcome the sin in their lives. They likely *fear* punishment—from God, from those they've hurt, and from the pseudo-pious. They also feel *shame* before God, before the people they know, and within themselves.

When spiritually sensitive people, especially Christians, sin, they feel personal guilt for several painful reasons:

- They know they have offended God.
- They know that "the wages of sin is death."[12]
- They have violated the standards and beliefs they personally hold sacred.
- They carry within a sense of failure before God and themselves.
- They live with the awareness that they have hurt people they love.

As bad as these awarenesses make us feel, God wants us to feel personal guilt. Why? Because personal guilt, though painful, provides a very effective warning system to steer us away from sin.

So, *why*, Lawrence wanted to know, didn't his guilt kick in until after the damage was done, after he'd made an absolute mess of his life? It didn't because he so intently pursued his sin that he blocked out all efforts to warn him of his impending spiritual disaster. The "ecstasy of love" proved too strong an elixir, intoxicating his usually rational way of thinking. Its anesthesia dulled him to the sinful scalpel carefully dissecting his spirit, body, and mind. Logical, practical Lawrence became an unthinking, helpless pawn in the hands of Satan.

The personal guilt God designed to stop us from continued sin was barred from his heart. It undoubtedly pounded and pleaded, demanding attention and correction of course, but Lawrence didn't hear. Feelings of overwhelming desire sufficiently dimmed the clamor from his conscience to make it nothing more than an annoying tap at the window. Only as passion crawled back into its lair, satisfied and indifferent, did Lawrence finally, belatedly, feel the self-preserving assault guilt had been making on his heart all along.

Like everyone who wants to do right, Lawrence eventually had to recognize the consequences of his behavior. Guilt had to consume him. His lover couldn't replace everything and everyone in his life. Neither could she help him continue to be the same man she'd fallen in love with. The very act of leaving his family for her contradicted the core values that made him who he was.

Most important, she couldn't replace the intimate relationship Lawrence once enjoyed with God.

THE GUILT MODEL

In my work as a consultant/trainer to corporate America before becoming president of Family Dynamic Institute, I learned that some concepts are easier to grasp when placed in a visual model. So I asked a Bible class at my home church to suggest potential models based on my short presentation of guilt and grace. Ray Sprankle, one of the class members, suggested an idea that served as the seed from which I developed what I call "The Guilt Model."

The model depicts four possible spiritual states in which you may operate. If you live above the horizontal line, you stand legally guilty before God, whether you realize it or not. If you are below that horizontal line, you are legally innocent in God's court, whether you realize it or not.

If you are to the right of the vertical line, you experience no personal guilt. Legally guilty or not, you feel no guilt. If you reside to the left of the vertical line, you do experience personal guilt—legally guilty or not, you feel personal guilt.

Deceived

Because they stand legally guilty before God but feel no personal guilt, the people in the upper right quadrant are spiritually deceived.

The deception may be lifelong and may keep a person out of heaven by keeping that person from becoming a Christian. Or the deception may be temporary, causing great spiritual harm but not ending in spiritual demise. Take Lawrence, for example. His adultery stood as a legal sin before God,[13] but Lawrence refused to admit it as sin. He divorced his wife so he could marry his lover—even though God plainly tells us that He hates divorce[14]—and convinced himself that wasn't sin either. He rationalized his legal sin so that he felt no personal guilt. He operated in the deceived spiritual state.

When Lawrence finally recognized his legal guilt, he felt personal guilt. That recognition moved him from the deceived state to the aware state. He remained deceived only as long as he refused to acknowledge either legal or personal guilt.

Aware

When people realize and accept their sins before God, they move into the upper left quadrant. They are aware of their guilt. The legal guilt that exists before God now also exists in their hearts. They finally hear the Holy Spirit's message convicting them of sin;[15] they become aware of their sin and want—usually desperately—to do something about their spiritual dilemma. They want guilt removed so they will no longer feel the turmoil and pain and can regain inner peace. That realization creates within them a brokenness that brings them humbly to the feet of God.[16] This brokenness is good, for it forces them to act in response to God's commands.

You likely have seen a person come into awareness—some call it "coming under conviction"—during a church service. I admit that I never cease to be amazed as I watch God bring people into awareness during revivals I preach for churches around the world. Sometimes I don't ask for the usual invitational hymn churches tend to use but just stop preaching and ask for those on whom God is working to join me at the front of the auditorium. I ask them to come and stand with me. Not those simply wishing to pray. Not those wishing others to pray for them. But those eaten up with guilt because they have become aware of their sin before God.

Some come because they want to be Christians. Others because they, like Lawrence, finally admit to themselves the guilt of their sins. I've seen a church leader hand over his crack pipe. A church secretary confess her immorality. A youth minister tell the whole church about his addiction to pornography. A father confess molesting his daughter. The list goes on and on. Some sins you might consider major and some you might think not quite so bad—but the sinners think they're bad. Some of the people who come tell the whole church what they've been convicted of. Others tell only counselors, who join them at the front later in the service.

Why would people take such risks and be so open?

Because a person who becomes aware must act.

Unlike the deceived, aware people won't stay in a spiritually static state. Deceived people feel no need to do anything about their spiritual state; aware people *have* to do something. Because their guilt forces them into some kind of action, they will necessarily move from this quadrant to one of the other three.

Some Are Healed

God wants to move aware people into the spiritually healed state. If aware people aren't Christians, realization of their sinfulness should lead them to place their faith in Jesus and surrender in lifelong obedience to Him. Like the Ethiopian eunuch rising from his baptismal waters, these new Christians would go on their ways rejoicing,[17] spreading the good news wherever they went. If they are Christians who finally realize the spiritual deception that led them to ignore the will of God, they will recommit their lives to the Lord. They know they can draw near to God with a sincere heart in full assurance of faith, for it is a heart cleansed from a guilty conscience.[18]

That's what is supposed to happen.

Sometimes it doesn't.

Some Return to Deception

Unfortunately, aware people may not move into the healed spiritual state. Instead they may move back into the deceived state. This occurs if they do not conquer the sin in their lives by the power of God. Such people will keep on sinning until their feelings of personal guilt pave over shame and the longing of the spirit for communion with God. They sin until their hearts become completely hardened. They recognize neither legal nor personal guilt.[19] As they move back into deceived from aware, they typically don't do it with the thought that God no longer holds their sins against them. No, they move back there not caring whether God holds their sins against them or not. They either convince themselves that there is no God or that they cannot please Him.

Some Become Guilt Caged

When Lawrence finally became aware of his sin before God, he needed to grasp God's power to overcome his sin. Otherwise, rather than his awareness drawing him closer to God, it could have easily convinced him he was beyond redemption. His lifestyle would have become dominated by hopelessness, and he would have moved into the guilt-caged spiritual state.

Guilt Caged

Those in the lower left quadrant of the model exist in the spiritual state I refer to as guilt caged. Even though God has forgiven their sin, these sinners hang on to the personally felt guilt. Like Rick in the first chapter, these Christians live in misery. They, too, are deceived, but in a different way. It's not their salvation that is in danger—it is their *joy*, their effectiveness in the kingdom. Satanic forces couldn't keep them from God, so, through lies, they are kept from enjoying God.

Sound like too small a goal for our spiritual enemies?

Think again.

Christians without joy are basically useless to the work of God. They will enter heaven when they die, but they will take no one with them. After all, who would want what they have? Can you picture an unbeliever saying to a miserable Christian, "I've been watching you, and I just have to know what makes you so unhappy. I want to follow your God so He can make me miserable too!"

Absolutely not!

Guilt-caged Christians live their lives in spiritual misery, and whether they mean to or not, they cast that spiritual shadow on others. They become thorns in the sides of some, roadblocks to the growth of the church (both evangelistically and spiritually), and spreaders of gloom and doom. I'm sure satanic forces have great fun watching the misery and pain these guilt-caged Christians inflict on others.

Oh, don't misunderstand me. If you are a guilt-caged Christian, I'm not trying to make you feel even worse. I'm simply describing why Satan wants to keep you in this sad spiritual state. I want to shine the light on his tactics. If this is your spiritual state, God wants to move you from this state into the spiritual state I call healed.

Healed

In the lower right quadrant is peace, harmony, and a fellowship with God. This is the state Isaiah described to the sinners of his day when he told them that even though God had seen their wickedness and had been enraged by it, He would give them a marvelous, grace-filled package if they would but turn their hearts back to Him.[20] As you recall from chapter 1, God offered several specific gifts in this passage:

- a new life (revival)
- a new condition (comfort)
- a new emotion (peace)
- a new direction (guidance)

Nearly everywhere I speak, people tell me they want something more from their spiritual lives. Recently, during a Sunday morning Bible class I taught at the beginning of a revival, I asked, "How many of you feel there is something more? Something you don't have that God is offering?" When hundreds of hands thrust into the air, I followed with, "What do you think that 'something' is?"

Answers varied slightly, but as they came from across the room, I heard the cry for the very blessings promised in Isaiah 57.

"I want fire in my spiritual life." *Revival.*

"I want a life much different from the one I have now. I want to overcome the stress, the misery, the complications." *Comfort and peace.*

"What I want more than anything is for God to let me know what He wants from me. What He wants me to be. Where He wants me to go. Who He wants me to be with." *Guidance.*

Though they don't realize it, they all want the very thing Isaiah promised. They want sin, guilt, doubt, fear, and every other negative thing removed so they can enjoy intimacy with God. They crave an intimacy that can only exist when a person knows there is nothing hindering his relationship with God.

Personally, I can't think of a better word to wrap all those blessings in than *healed.* Through Isaiah God says, "I will heal you." Sin is a disease, and guilt is one of its consequences, and we desperately need *healing* from this deadly disease.

Healed Christians know that they occasionally sin, though they try with all their surrendered hearts not to.[21] They pray regularly, commune with God by letting Him speak to them through His Word, and allow God to work through them in His way.[22] They feel neither spiritual arrogance nor spiritual shame. They know they are forgiven, and they find joy in that salvation. They know that no sin sticks to them, that they are forgiven constantly and completely.[23]

They are forgiven twenty-four hours a day.

Seven days a week.

Three hundred sixty-five days a year.

For all the years of the rest of their lives.

Of course, this is where you want to be. And this is where you can be by the time you finish this book.

If you let God take you there.

By now you can see that personal guilt is good. And that personal guilt is bad. It is within your power to choose which it will be for you.

People can become numb to feelings of guilt before God, but they can never remove the reality of the guilt. Only people who come to an awareness of their guilt and look to God for healing will experience true healing, for spiritual healing exists only in the grace of God.

If, like Lawrence, you've already moved from deception to awareness, there is hope for you. You may be unable to get back all you've sacrificed for your sin. God made it clear that we often reap what we sow, that we receive the consequences of our actions.[24]

Or He *may* restore to you what you lost by your sin. He did for me and for many others. I hope He does for you. But remember this: You have no right to demand it. He has the right to remain silent as you request it. Whether He restores what you've lost or not, there is one thing He will definitely do for you. He *will* heal you of all sin—even sin that you have refused to recognize until now.

God offers freedom from both types of guilt—legal and personal. Your job is to acknowledge your guilt and seek His healing power.

When we sin, we incur legal guilt, which affects God's relationship with each part of us. When we realize our sin, we experience personal guilt, which affects the relationship God has with each part of us.

Restore to me the joy of your salvation and grant me a willing spirit, to sustain me.

Psalm 51:12

3

How Does Guilt Affect Me?

I sat in the examination room trembling more from fear than the inevitable antiseptic chill. I kept my eyes on the book in my lap, maintaining my courage by refusing to acknowledge the gleaming implements of torture and healing lining the counter. From the corner of my eye I could see the cotton balls in a large jar next to the sink watching sadly as they silently waited with me. It was as if they knew but were too polite to mention it. I was in trouble. Serious trouble. And I didn't know what to do.

Daniel knocked and paused for a quarter-beat before he was blown through the door by that gust of energy perpetually propelling him. My wife, Alice, had discovered him when I called home from a seminar I was doing in Phoenix for a gathering of Sears, Roebuck, & Co. trainers. I told her I simply had to find another doctor; the current one was failing me. My criteria were simple: Find a physician who is young but experienced, brilliant but caring, and confident but humble. Oh, and by the way, he or she would positively have to be able to heal me.

Alice found Daniel Boone.

Really.

A descendant of the famous pioneer, Dr. Boone had come highly recommended. Alice informed me, "He breezed through medical school with a 4.0. He's young enough to be up on all the new information and old enough to have experience." Alice didn't know it then, but Daniel also loves the Lord Jesus. I'm sure that's why God sent me to him.

And now I sat in his examination room waiting for him to tell me the results of the myriad of recently completed medical tests. For several months, my health had deteriorated so rapidly that I could hardly work. Because I could not be on my feet all day, my seminar business was slowly crumbling around me, and financial chaos loomed near. I'd already lost my health insurance. The only thing I could still depend on was God, and I felt He was too disappointed with me to lift a divine finger in my defense.

Daniel talked for a few moments about test results, concluding with, "One test pointed to lupus, but I'm sure that was a 'red herring.'" He then cleared his throat and uttered the most remarkable words I'd ever heard from a medical doctor. "Joe, I'm convinced you're under spiritual attack. I believe your physical problems are the result of a spiritual dilemma. You are sick. But your sickness won't be cured by medicine. It will be cured only by God. You must let God heal you."

As quickly as his words found me, I knew in my heart they were right. But my muddled thinking couldn't sort everything out, so I responded dully, "What do you mean?"

"Your sickness emanates from guilt. Evil forces are using your guilt to destroy you. In order for your body to be healed, you must first be healed of your guilt . . . and only God can do that."

That day Daniel set me on a path that affected me for eternity, and I want to share with you what I learned. But to understand the solution, we must more clearly comprehend the problem. The next step toward finding God's healing is understanding how guilt affects each part of our beings—even our physical health.

OUR TRINARY NATURE

Before delving deeper into our study, we need to briefly examine the trinary nature of humankind. We can't find answers to such questions as, "Why do I feel so guilty?" and "How can I find healing?" until we understand how guilt affects every part of us. That's right—every part of us. Many of the principles explained here find their simplest expression in the awareness that we are trinary—that is, we exist in three parts. If you really want a deeper insight into yourself, your sin, and your guilt, it is vital to master this concept.

We humans consist of three inseparable components. We are *body*, meaning we are physical bodies, of flesh and blood.[1] We are *mind*, meaning we are both intellectual and emotional.[2] And we are *spirit*, meaning there is a part of us that was formed within us by God Himself.[3]

The following model represents how these three parts make up our whole.[4]

The Trinary Model

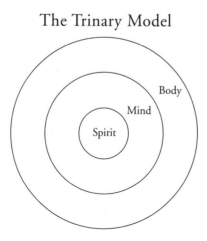

As far as I can tell, each is as much a part of us as the other. In my younger days I argued that our spiritual dimension superseded everything else, but years of study and learning have moderated that view. While it is true that the spiritual dimension is at our core, our inmost being, the spirit does not and cannot live on this earth without joint partnership with both mind and body.

Everything we do affects and is affected by these three components of ourselves. Work, family, dining habits, prayer, worship, recreation, self-worth—everything. These three dimensions represent the complex beings we are.

Ready to think this through?

Since the body is the "outer person," it would seem the appropriate place to begin our study. But I prefer to begin with the mind. Understanding the parts of the mind expands our model to make matters of the body and spirit clearer.

The Mind

The mind consists of two components that combine to compose the third:

1. The *intellect* thinks logically. It processes information and compares it to previous experiences and core values.
2. The *emotions* feel a spectrum of sensations both through mental and physical stimulation.
3. The *heart* is where the intellect and mind come together to form the center of a person's reasoning, the point where decisions are made and actions are taken.[5]

When you experience personal guilt, your mind feels the brunt of it in all three places—intellect, emotions, and reasoning (heart).

Intellect

It isn't difficult to understand the guilt you intellectually acknowledge when you know you have sinned. Intellectually, you know and understand what you have done and the consequences of those actions before God, in your life, and in the lives of those you love.

Of course, the guilt hits hard. Once you recognize your sin and its consequences, it is nearly impossible to continue in the behavior that violates the value system you believe. The mental dissonance is just too overwhelming. When you finally acknowledge your sin, your mind reacts strongly to the awareness. Either you must change your beliefs and values, or you must abandon the discordant actions.

Most Christians can continue in sin only as long as they compartmentalize their thinking, shutting off some thoughts from others so they don't have to admit to themselves their incongruity. That happened with me. When I sinned as a preacher, I never thought about my sin while preparing my sermons or while preaching them. Nor did I think about my beliefs or quote passages while I sinned.

But when we accept personal guilt, we can no longer hide from ourselves.

When you finally come to acceptance, you tend to think yourself the least intelligent person on the planet. You doubt your life, your decisions, and your ability to reason.

I'll never forget the thought that kept running through my mind the night I lay in intensive care, waiting to die the death of a fool. With disgust, I said it to myself over and over.

"What a stupid way to die."

Emotions

Most of us understand that personal guilt affects our emotions. When we acknowledge the guilt before God, we feel a pain within that tears at the fabric of our being.

Some months ago I sat in a room with a couple of church leaders who had been summoned, along with me, to the home of a couple in great distress. The husband had heard me preach in a revival at his church and had let God's Word penetrate his heart. Overcome with guilt, he confessed years of secret sin to his wife.

Intellectually, he bore the brunt of his guilt.

But the process wasn't finished. He hadn't yet allowed himself to feel the emotion.

As the church leaders prayed with him, I sat watching. He and I were the only two in the room with our eyes open while fervent prayers lifted from loving men. He didn't pray; he watched me. I prayed, but I watched him. During the whole time of prayer, we never broke eye contact.

His hurting intellect finally spoke, "I think I'm evil." He said it without emotion. Without voice inflection. Empty and flat.

I replied, "You may be. I don't know. But God can tell you if you are. Why don't you pray now and ask Him if you are."

"I can't pray."

"Sure you can. You mean that you don't want to pray, don't want to talk with God because you feel nothing. Just address Him and ask, 'Am I an evil man? Speak to my heart.'"

After several moments of silence, he bowed slightly and asked God that all important question. He didn't pray long. The answer I expected came rather quickly. He started to sob, escalating into a wail, and finally lost all strength in his body. He slumped from the sofa onto the floor, weeping uncontrollably.

Clinging to his wife, who fell to the floor beside him and held him as if he were her child, he mourned his sin.

What was his sin?

It doesn't matter.

When he came to the awareness of his sin—personally accepting his guilt—he couldn't stand before God any longer. It doesn't have to be a scandal, some sin that evokes shock. Any sin that makes a person realize his guilt before God can do it.

For example, what do you think Peter felt so guilty about that he couldn't stand any longer, couldn't face Jesus, but instead fell and implored, "Go away from me, Lord; I am a sinful man!"[6]

Facing any guilt can do that.

Unresolved personal guilt will lead your emotions to destroy your body.

Emotionally, you feel the pain of guilt, and it eats at you from the inside.

And I do mean *eat*.

Many people feel the effects of guilt in their stomachs, in the form of excess acid that eats away at them from the inside. The longer the guilt lasts, the more damage it does.

Reasoning

Guilt also works its evil on your heart, your center of reasoning, and your reasoning becomes confused in at least three ways.[7]

First, this guilt confusion sometimes leads Christians to condemn even the slightest offenses of others.[8] Those who feel the greatest burden of sin sometimes season their guilt by highlighting the sins of other saints.[9] Every time I encounter a bitter Christian who seems compelled to find and publicize faults—real or imagined—I find myself wondering what guilt drives him to such spiritual madness.

Other confused Christians internalize their guilt so that it attacks them. When this happens, they become prisoners of depression, anxiety, and fear. Like King David, they experience such self-condemnation that they exaggeratedly think they were evil from the time they first drew breath, or even before: "Surely I was sinful at birth, sinful from the time my mother conceived me."[10] Their sins haunt them day and night: "For I know my transgressions, and my sin is always before me."[11] And, like David, they fear God's abandonment because of His disgust with their heinous behavior.[12]

Finally, when not dealt with properly, guilt can so confuse Christians' hearts that they are no longer subject to God's leading—neither from the Word nor through the Holy Spirit's guidance in their lives. And without God's direction, doubts and sin invariably creep in. Doubt that they can maintain their relationship with God. Doubt that God even wants to continue the relationship. And, finally, doubt that God is even there. Doubt drains power from the Word so that it loses its ability to penetrate.[13] And sin takes such a hold that Christians spiral slowly into a cesspool where God's voice fades, and they hopelessly resign themselves to yielding to temptation. They no longer listen for the voice of God, and they cease praying, feeling that surely God doesn't want to hear from such evil sinners. Slowly, inexorably, they give up, and they sin without inner struggle. Intellectually they admit their sins, but they feel no remorse. They no longer resemble the Christians they once were.

This isn't what God designed guilt to do.

It's a satanic perversion.

When Satan's forces twist personal guilt to their own use, they alter the very guilt that God designed to stop us from sin and make it an ally of sin in the minds and hearts of struggling Christians.

The Body

When we experience guilt, we may experience its effects in our bodies just as we do in our minds. King David did. Referring to the guilt he felt before God because of his adultery with Bathsheba and the murder of her husband, Uriah, David used phrases like, "my bones wasted away"[14] and "the bones you have crushed."[15] He suffered physical consequences from his personal guilt.

You may too.

As guilt festers, it begins to eat away at our bodies. Sickness, both real and imagined, as well as a predisposition to accidents, sometimes appears in those who feel great personal guilt. Guilt, working on its host, not only weakens the body but may cause such turmoil that the body actually begins to attack itself. A myriad of studies now tells us of the risk to health and life caused by stress. Personal guilt is a kind of stress that probably supersedes any other stress a person may face.

Even legal guilt—guilt that may not be felt emotionally—can affect our bodies. Sin can cause sickness even before an individual consciously accepts the reality of the sin. A sexually transmitted disease, for example, doesn't need the host's awareness of sinfulness to take root in the body. Similarly, those who refuse to acknowledge sin on a conscious level may punish themselves physically because of a subconscious awareness of sin. These people know they're getting sick—or sicker—but they don't recognize that subconscious guilt is driving that sickness. They don't recognize it because they don't acknowledge their guilt.

Do you doubt this could happen?

Before you reject physical deterioration because of sin as nonsense, consider again that you are mind, body, and spirit. Each component is inseparable from the other, and each affects the other. When one part of your being enjoys health, it brings health to the other parts. When one part gets sick, the other parts may get sick as well. A review of Solomon's writings on the matter demonstrates that the Holy Spirit acknowledges the interaction of the parts of a man:

- "A heart at peace gives life to the body, but envy rots the bones."[16]
- "A happy heart makes the face cheerful, but heartache crushes the spirit."[17]
- "A cheerful heart is good medicine, but a crushed spirit dries up the bones."[18]

Obviously, Solomon saw a direct correlation between the mind, body, and spirit. He made it very clear that each affects the health and well-being of the other. Because that correlation exists, those who sin sometimes experience physical manifestations of their sins.

Maybe you should stop here and spend a few moments in reflection about your own pain, depression, or sickness. Yes, it is very true that sickness and degeneration are part of our fallen world. Genetic flaws, predisposition to certain diseases, susceptibility to contagion, and the weakening of the body as it ages all result from Eve and Adam's sin.[19] There may be a definite cause for your sickness that has nothing to do with sin. And if that is the case, please don't let anything I write be used by satanic forces to make you feel false guilt. But . . . make sure that you haven't accepted some satanic lie that blames someone or something else for your own consequences. Some people are depressed because of their own sin—even if they refuse to admit that sin. Some are sick or accident prone or aging faster than they should because of guilt—even repressed or subconscious guilt. For example, I know from personal experience that depression and a sense of worthlessness can spring from spiritual rebellion that we don't have the courage to admit to ourselves. And I learned from Dr. Daniel Boone that guilt can affect our minds and bodies to the extent that our immune systems falter, making us vulnerable to whatever germs or ailments are passing by.

Guilt can kill you.

Literally.

But don't panic. There's good news. If you experience physical distress because of your sin and guilt, there will be an extra blessing in this book for you. With the healing of your guilt, you may also receive the subsequent healing of the manifestations of that guilt in your body. Spiritual healing may bring you physical healing.

The Spirit

Your spirit is the very essence of who you are. It is your spirit that separates you from the animals; it is your spirit that identifies you as one made in the image of God.

There is much current interest and speculation regarding the spiritual nature of man, and there are also many misconceptions. While the Bible may not answer all our questions, it gives us valuable insights:

- You are spirit because God is spirit[20] and because you are made in His likeness.[21]
- Your spirit is the core of your inmost being: "The lamp of the Lord searches the spirit of a man; it searches out his inmost being."[22]
- Unless your spirit has been dwarfed by continual sin, your spirit desires Him—"My soul yearns for you in the night; in the morning my spirit longs for you"[23]— and worships Him gladly.[24]
- Your spirit gives life to your body, and without its presence your body cannot live.[25]

- Since your spirit is the core of who you are, it understands you like no other person can. "For who among
men knows the thoughts of a man except the man's
spirit within him?"[26]

In addition to your own spirit, if you are a Christian, you also
have the Spirit of God living in your inner being with your spirit.[27]
God strengthens you "with power through His Spirit in your inner
being." And through your spirit, God makes known to you things
that those without Him can neither appreciate nor understand.[28]
Because your spirit is so closely tied to your Creator, when you sin
against Him, your spirit experiences immediate consequences.
Because Christians are one in spirit with the Lord,[29] when you sin,
you wound His Spirit. When you violate His law, you violate Him,
the lawmaker. The close communion between you and God strains
as you violate His very essence. He is holy, and holiness is the
antithesis of sin. The damage you do to your relationship through
sin damages your spirit. This occurs at the inception of legal guilt,
before you ever feel personal guilt. But when the personal guilt
descends on you, you realize you have damaged your spiritual relationship with God and you long to restore it.

A sin-damaged spirit craves "renewing," "steadfastness," and a
"willingness" that sustains.[30] It wants reassurance that the Holy
Spirit of God will not depart.[31] For that very reason, God wants
your spirit to feel its sinfulness. He desires brokenness before Him
because it makes us long even more deeply for Him. It also makes
us much more aware of the things we do that offend Him.

I'd like you to stop reading for a few moments and spend the
next few minutes praying and meditating on the following passages. They will help you understand God's desire for you to feel
broken before Him.

The Lord is close to the brokenhearted and saves those who are crushed in spirit.[32]

The sacrifices of God are a broken spirit; a broken and contrite heart, O God, you will not despise.[33]

For this is what the high and lofty One says—he who lives forever, whose name is holy: "I live in a high and holy place, but also with him who is contrite and lowly in spirit, to revive the spirit of the lowly and to revive the heart of the contrite."[34]

Body, mind, spirit—each is a part of the other.

Even though I have written about this trinary nature as if each part were separate, that isn't how it works. It's just the easiest way to explain the parts. In actuality, each is inextricable from the others. They remain interconnected for as long as we are alive. Each part affects the others, yet often one part will command more influence on the whole being than another part. For example, when we walk by "flesh" (KJV) or "sinful nature" (NIV), we allow the body to have more control than the spirit. If, on the other hand, we walk by the Spirit, we allow our spirits to exert more control on our lives than our sinful natures.[35]

GUILT AFFECTS EVERY PART OF US

Sin strongly affects the mind, the body, and the spirit. When we sin, we incur legal guilt, which affects God's relationship with each part of us. When we realize our sin, we experience personal guilt, which affects the relationship each part of us has with God.

I was at this point when God, through Alice, sent me to Dr. Daniel Boone.

A few years earlier, I'd committed the most terrible sin of my life. By the standards of this world, many people wouldn't think it sinful at all. But I did. I still do. And the pain of it was killing me—physically, mentally, and spiritually.

Many times I'd begged God to forgive me. I understood the concept of grace and had preached it for many years in many places. But because of a powerful sense of personal guilt, I couldn't accept it for myself. I felt deeply in my heart that because I knew better and had sinned so selfishly and so brazenly, God might not forgive me. I quoted Scripture to other people to convince them that God forgave even their most heinous actions, but sadly, I couldn't accept those same verses myself. More than once I wished for the same belief I was able to plant in others.

I knew I felt guilt. I just didn't yet realize it was guilt that was driving my physical deterioration as well as my distrust of people and myself. Daniel had to show me that. And from there I had to learn how to allow God to heal me—not just physically, but first and foremost, from my personally felt guilt. I had to allow Him to heal my spirit, my mind, and my body. My personal guilt had manifested itself in all three.

If your body shows signs of sin's effects, it may be that when God heals your guilt, your body may be healed as well. Or it may be that, for God's own purposes, He won't give complete physical healing. But you should seek that healing. While God is sovereign and does as He wishes, there often appears to be a direct correlation between the healing of guilt and the healing of physical problems.[36]

Are you beginning to understand how guilt affects all three parts of you and why you feel so guilty when you know you sin? Are you beginning to get an idea of how God will heal your guilt and restore close communion with Him?

You will. Keep reading.

Deliverance from powerful temptation comes only when God's Spirit, working through a person's spirit, overcomes the flesh.

❧

For in my inner being I delight in God's law; but I see another law at work in the members of my body, waging war against the law of my mind and making me a prisoner of the law of sin at work within my members.

Romans 7:22

CHAPTER

Why Do I Sin?

"Your deacon is drunk again, and God only knows where he is!" Cecelia hurled the words at me through the phone, venom dripping from every syllable. I didn't make a sound in response. I didn't know what to say. Our church had shown extraordinary patience with Ned, and we'd thought that by prayer, patience, and the power of God he'd mastered the inner demon that drove him to drunkenness.

Apparently we'd underestimated the power that demon wielded.

"He called me from Chicago, slurring so bad I could barely understand him. He said they served cocktails at the business meeting. Said he was sure he could stop with just one. Yeah, that's what he said, 'Stop with just one.' He couldn't drink just one if his children's lives depended on it.

"Now he's at O'Hare airport, with a pocket full of company credit cards, so drunk he's babbling out of his mind. He could fly anywhere in the world and wake up in a couple of days not even knowing where he is or how he got there. I'm worried sick. And furious at myself for even caring. I can't take this . . . I can't live like this. You hear me? I can't!"

And with that, Cecelia slammed the receiver down.

I considered calling back to try to diffuse some of her anger but decided the better course of action was to find her husband. I found an operator who could give me Yellow Page listings in Chicago and rapidly jotted the phone numbers of hotels around O'Hare airport on the back of a handy envelope.

It took only minutes to discover that none of them registered Ned as a guest.

Choosing a few airports that receive direct flights from Chicago, I repeated the process.

No Ned.

Again and again I tried, until I finally had to admit the futility of searching for a drunk, unreasoning man who could be in any one of a thousand hotels in any one of a hundred cities.

Thinking maybe Cecelia had calmed enough that I could minister to her, I gave her a call. No, she hadn't heard from Ned. No, she didn't want to talk. No, she wasn't going to bed to try to get some sleep, and what kind of an idiot was I to suggest she try?

I didn't call again.

And I didn't sleep too well either.

The next morning, my work at the church office wasn't the best of my ministry. Nothing is more frustrating than wanting to help and not having a clue what to do. As I pondered, the clue walked into my office.

"Ned! Where have you been?"

"Here . . . in town, I mean. I flew in from Chicago last night and stayed at a motel near the airport."

I briefly considered choking him but decided I wouldn't be able to adequately explain my actions at the next deacons' meeting. I asked lamely, "Been home yet?"

"No." He attempted a very tired smile through his bloated, blotched face. But the smile rose no higher than his lips; resignation and pain brimmed in his bloodshot eyes. "I think that's the one place I can't go. I don't have the backbone to face Cecelia and the kids. She's already called my boss and most likely got me fired. She knows I'm in town. She knows I'm alive. I think that's enough for now. But there's something I need from you, if you don't mind and can give it."

That's what I wanted to hear. At last there would be something I could do! "You got it! Whadaya' need?"

"Tell me," he said as he sagged into a chair across from my desk, "why I keep doing this when I know what it'll cost me?"

"Take your time. I got all day."

If you've ever found yourself struggling repeatedly with a recurring temptation, you've probably asked the same question Ned asked me. Why do I keep doing things I know will hurt me spiritually, mentally, emotionally, and physically? Surely, in the scheme of things, sin shouldn't have that kind of power over anyone. So why does it sometimes seem so overwhelmingly powerful?[1]

In the previous chapter, we saw how sin and guilt affect each part of us. But if you think this new knowledge will prevent you from sinning, think again.

The question remains, Why do we sin?

The answer lies in the trinary model introduced in chapter 3. Temptation comes at us through each of our trinary parts, with the strongest temptations coming through the flesh. But flesh can only get its way when it coerces the cooperation of the mind and spirit.

THE WEAKNESS OF THE FLESH

The King James Version translates the Greek word *sarx* as "flesh," while the New International Version translates it "sinful nature." "In Paul's thought especially, the flesh is the willing instrument of sin, and is subject to sin to such a degree that wherever flesh is, all forms of sin are likewise present, and no good thing can live in the 'sarx.' "[2]

The word *sarx* is used in the New Testament sometimes to refer simply to the body.[3] But as inspired by the Holy Spirit, Paul wrote that the body isn't just what we live in; flesh also carries appetites and lusts of its own, and they are predominantly bad.[4]

What kind of appetites and lusts?

There are at least three strong self-directed drives inherit in a body of flesh and blood that can lead to selfish sin. They are the flesh's extreme intent on self-gratification, self-preservation, and self-perpetuation.

Self-gratification is the drive to find as much pleasure, comfort, and satisfaction as possible. While not always sinful, this drive often leads to sinful attitudes and actions. It shows itself in sins like greed, vanity, and self-centeredness. It also leads to the strong drive that many—if not most—people feel to control their lives and the things and people who touch their lives.

Self-preservation is the drive to extend one's own life. At face value this drive certainly doesn't appear sinful. But it can and will lead to sin when the desire to extend one's own life so permeates that a person becomes focused on earthly matters to the neglect of spiritual matters.[5]

Self-perpetuation is the drive to produce offspring to continue one's own bloodline, giving the person a sense of continued existence after death. Self-perpetuation's most obvious manifestation is the sex drive, but at heart, it goes much deeper than merely wanting sex. For example, just as in the animal kingdom the drive to attract a suitable mate leads animals to fight, display gaudy behavior, and do all sorts of things to attract the attention of the opposite sex, so it is with humans. I believe that for many people the drive for power, prestige, accolades, riches, and the like aren't always driven just by the need for self-gratification. They may be more often driven by the drive for self-perpetuation; a human's way of doing the same things done by other animals to attract as many potential partners as possible.

While none of these three drives is inherently evil, each is so strong that it carries great weakness to enticement to evil. Notice that at the core of each drive is the element of self.

Those selfish elements *in* flesh stand synonymous *with* flesh. The human body itself is not evil, but the sinful nature that comes from living in a human body is subject to evil at all times.

As long as we live in this body, we will be subject to sin—whether we like it or not. Since the flesh has such power, we need to know more about its appetite.

Paul talks extensively about our body's sinful nature in Romans 7 and 8 and in Galatians 5. If you understand Paul's nature, you won't be surprised that God used him to pen these discourses. Paul would have understood Ned's struggle—the same struggle many of us face, though each of us faces it through different temptations. Paul, too, struggled with wanting to do one thing while doing another. "I do not understand what I do. For what I want to do I do not do, but what I hate I do . . . the evil I do not want to do—this I keep on doing."[6]

In my office that day, I opened the Scripture and read Ned that passage. "You ever feel like that?"

You know he said yes.

You probably find those feelings familiar also.

Of course, hearing Paul's confession did little to help Ned with his struggle. While it encouraged him to know that a person as godly as Paul felt what he felt, Ned wanted more than empathy. He wanted answers. Perhaps you want those same answers. As we seek the cure, we discover that through Paul God made clear the cause of the disease. He says of his struggle, "I know that nothing good lives in me, that is, in my sinful nature."[7]

There it is, that word *sarx* that refers to our body's desire for sin. It's the cause of our troubles. Satan attacks the flesh, and the flesh attacks the mind.

The flesh attacks the mind?

Yes. Paul goes on to say about the body: "I see another law at work in the members of my body, waging war against the law of my mind and making me a prisoner of the law of sin at work within my members."[8] He actually pictures the body and mind at war with each other. The mind can know what God desires. It can even know the consequences of sin. It definitely abhors the pain brought on by legal or personal guilt. But the flesh can be so overpowering that it simply defeats the mind in the battle for control of a person's life.

How would an artist draw such a battle? If you're the creative type, maybe you can sketch it. If you do, send me a copy. I'd love to see it. Having no artistic ability, I don't even know how to mentally picture it. The mind is a part of the body. So how can it be at battle with the body? Obviously, Paul isn't describing the brain crossing swords with the forearm. He's discussing the desires of the flesh in conflict with the desires of the mind, particularly the emotional part of the mind.

Surely you've experienced this, at least on some level. So many Christians have.

At one weekend retreat, I offered all present an opportunity to talk in small groups about any spiritual struggles they faced. After each person who wished to share did so, someone in the group would pray for victory in that person's life. As we listened and prayed, one young Christian woman in the group would occasionally lean over and whisper in my ear, "I don't know why I'm here. I don't have any great struggles."

Around the fifth time she said that, I braced myself for whatever sin she must be desperately wanting to share. Finally, just as the group was about to disperse, she blurted, "I need your prayers. I so much want to be a dedicated Christian woman, but that is so hard to do when you're single, wanting a godly husband, but thinking you may grow old alone. I'm not as young as I used to be, not as attractive. With all my heart I seek Jesus, but something strong within me wants something else. It just wants to be loved. To be held. To *not* be alone. I teach class at my church. Play a leading role in our singles group. But I feel like that's such a sham. I can't begin to tell you how many men there have been. Sometimes Christian men. Sometimes godless men. I feel so cheap and so dirty, but no matter how much I tell myself it will never happen again . . . it always does.

"Oh, God have mercy on my soul! Please pray that somehow I can overcome this sin. That I can be who I want to be."

In the war for control of self, the sinful nature's passions can overpower the mind and completely control a person.[9]

THE BATTLE FOR THE MIND

Maybe you know the passages about having a renewed mind[10] or setting your mind on things above.[11] Having God transform us by renewing our minds is crucial because a mind turned from God to its own desires eventually becomes depraved, allowing—or even encouraging—actions that God finds abominable.[12]

If you think you would never allow yourself to become abominable to God, you are proven wrong every time you sin. Our minds will lead us from God when our flesh focuses on earthly things. That's what Jesus said happened to Peter: "Get behind me, Satan! You are a stumbling block to me; you do not have in mind the things of God, but the things of men."[13]

Jesus feared His impending crucifixion, knowing that much more than physical death would take place on that cross. Who better to share His fears and anxieties with than the three men who had become His best friends on earth—Peter, James, and John.

As He shared what He must suffer at the hands of the elders, chief priests, and scribes, He told his friends the end of the matter.

He would soon die.

That bit of news didn't sit well with Peter. Not just because He loved Jesus, but because it would interfere with the expectations he held of what Jesus was to accomplish. Already he'd been arguing with James and John about their respective positions in Jesus' kingdom once He'd done away with Roman oppression. A premature death on Jesus' part would not allow his dream to be fulfilled. Without a moment's hesitation, he decided to force his agenda on the Lord of all. "Peter took him aside and began to rebuke him. 'Never, Lord!' he said. 'This shall never happen to you!' "[14] Takes some kind of courage to rebuke God, doesn't it? Telling Him it will "never" happen when He told you it would?

No. It doesn't take courage at all. Not if your mind has been so defeated by your flesh that it doesn't think through what it is doing.

If Peter, one of Jesus' best friends, suffered a "mind defeat" because of his flesh, you can be certain it can happen to you too.

Your sinful nature, like Peter's, seeks what it wants and tries its best to focus your mind—both its intellect and emotion—on the things your flesh desires. "Well then," you may be thinking, "I'll just discipline myself to keep my mind pure, and I'll never sin!" Great idea. The problem is that it doesn't work. You cannot overcome your flesh by will power or positive thinking.

Why?

Because, quite simply, your flesh can outmaneuver your mind.

Temptation Traps

Have you ever ambled along, blissfully unaware that you were walking into a "temptation trap"? One minute you were just minding your own business and the next moment, right in front of you, stood a powerful temptation. A temptation that evoked all kinds of urges and attraction and desires.

I think that's what happened to King David on that fateful night he couldn't sleep. You know the story; it's in 2 Samuel 11. If you asked him why he couldn't sleep that night, I don't know what he would answer. Maybe he'd say he felt guilty over having sent his army to war rather than going along with them. Maybe the royal chef put too much spice in the mutton. Or maybe he just found the fragrances of spring drifting through his bedroom window too appealing and decided to sit in the moonlight and allow the aroma to wash over him.

From reading the story, I think the likely reason he couldn't sleep is that satanic forces were luring him into a "temptation trap."

They couldn't force David to sin, just like they cannot force you or me to sin, but they surely could lure him to the right place at the right time to do the wrong thing.

And so David walked on his roof, restless.

Unfortunately for him, he wasn't the only one up.

Bathsheba couldn't sleep either. Apparently she thought she could relax herself into sleepiness by taking a slow, luxurious bath in her backyard. It's not likely she thought that immodest. Almost surely the yard was fenced, and it was late at night, so she simply moved her bath closer to the scents of springtime flowers and vines. She needed no light; the moon would be enough. With no torch and such a late hour, who could see her? Her only risk was if someone walked from David's bedroom onto the roof, and that was unlikely because for some time now there had been no light showing from the king's quarters.

So she bathed in the moonlight.

And he watched from the shadows.

Satanic forces maneuvered two people into the right place at the right time to do the wrong thing.

David found himself mesmerized by a face that must have caused the stars to avert their eyes in recognition of her greater beauty. Moonlight. Springtime. And a forbidden vision of female loveliness that even the greatest sculptor could work years in vain to capture.[15]

If David had admitted the desire burning in his flesh but turned and walked wistfully to his bedroom to spend the night alone, what spiritual man would refuse to admire him? I would raise my voice in praise of his spiritual strength. Not every man is attracted so strongly to a passing princess, but some are.

David definitely was.

He sent for her. She came. They sinned.

If you know the story, you know the terrible consequences of that one night of yielding to fleshly pleasure. David's adultery rapidly deteriorated into more heinous sin. Trying to hide his impregnation of Bathsheba, he premeditatedly had Uriah, her husband, murdered.[16]

When confronted by the prophet Nathan, David blindly named his own punishment of a fourfold payback. He didn't realize he was setting his sad future, but that's just what happened. First the illegitimate son he fathered with Bathsheba died.[17] Later David's son Amnon raped his half-sister Tamar. David's beautiful, innocent daughter became a desolate woman.[18] In revenge, Tamar's full brother Absalom murdered Amnon.[19] Finally, Absalom was killed while trying to wrest the kingdom from his father, David.[20]

Three dead sons. One ruined daughter.

Appalling consequences. Horrible consequences. Unbearable consequences.

Why Do We Do It?

If we could interview David about his life, certainly we would ask, "Why, David? Why did you commit adultery with Bathsheba? You knew better. God even referred to you as a man with a heart like His. Please help us understand. Why did you do it?"

How do you think he would reply? I've thought about it a lot; not just from David's standpoint but also from my own. I, too, have sinned when I knew better. Like David, I've suffered painful consequences. Appalling consequences. Sometimes I run a movie in my mind of an interview with David, trying to understand myself by understanding him.

I'm not sure David could articulate his response. He could stammer, ramble, and probably hit on a reason or two. But if he's anything like me, or like the people I deal with regularly who struggle with sin, he would have a difficult time explaining it to his own satisfaction, much less to ours.

He might answer, "I don't know why I did it. I mean . . . I love God, and I want to serve Him. He's been so good to me . . . brought me from a shepherd boy to a king . . . given me just about anything a man could ask for. It wasn't because I didn't love God or didn't want to do right.

"I don't know . . . it's just . . . you should have seen her that night. It was like a dream come true. I couldn't help myself. I watched her, and the longer I watched her, the more I wanted her. Finally I just stopped thinking. No reason. No logic. All I could think was, 'Find that woman and get her!' I was so out of control I even asked the people close to me to find out who she was and bring her to me.

"I felt no embarrassment at the time. Just lust. But, no, I wouldn't say it was just lust. When she came to my palace, we talked. She wasn't just beautiful; she was smart and funny and caring . . . and understanding. I knew I wanted her, but it became much more than that. We connected. It was as if we were meant for each other."

He might conclude with the plea, "Does this make any sense to you at all?"

And those of us who have been so compelled by a sin—any sin—would have to answer, yes, we understand. We would know what David meant, even though he couldn't explain it. We can't explain it either.

Why is that? Why can't we explain what happens to us?

Because we don't sin logically. Spiritual people don't wake up one morning and say, "What can I do wrong today? Let me see . . . hmm. Yes. That's it. Now I need to plan it so it can be done by midnight!" Children of God don't sin because they want to do evil. They sin because the flesh overpowers the resolve of the mind to do right.

The Process of Mind Defeat

The process goes something like this:

1. Fleshly temptation ambushes you.

Temptations that create great fleshly desire within you ambush you through some "temptation trap." If that temptation is a new one—meaning the temptation isn't to a repetitive sin—you think yourself in control.

2. You agree with your flesh to "think" about it.

Confronted with the temptation, you realize its pull and know you must leave immediately. But as you turn to walk away, the flesh whispers, "Can't I just think about this?"

The flesh loves to impede a person's escape.

If you stop to think, the battle is nearly over. The flesh seduces the mind with thoughts like, "Why walk away so quickly? I know I don't want to do this, and surely I won't, but that doesn't mean I have to be in such a hurry. I'll stay just a little longer and enjoy as much of it as I can without really doing anything."

3. Emotions join flesh and entice you with possibilities.

Enjoying proximity with the temptation, all the while certain you won't sin, gives time for your flesh to enlist the aid of your emotions. Now the inner conversation advances toward its goal: "You know, doing this would be exciting. I know I'd like it if I did it. And this is probably the only time in my whole life I will ever have this opportunity. If I walk away, I may never have this chance again! Can I live with the knowledge that I could have . . . just this once . . . but didn't? Leave now and I'll regret it for the rest of my life."

4. Your Spirit weakens and your flesh gains control.

The power of your spirit weakens as your flesh gains more control. Your spirit, listening to the Spirit of God, wants to flee. But your mind, drugged by the passion growing in your flesh and emotions, now wants to find a lie to believe so you can commit the sin. You subconsciously look for any rationalization, anything that will help you justify experiencing this sin.

5. Your mind joins your flesh and rationalizes.

At this point, your mind has joined the sin process. It thinks something like this: "I know this is wrong, but I very much want to experience it . . . to feel it just this once. Surely God, in His great mercy, can forgive me just this one time. I know He will."

Or your mind may try to convince you of an even greater lie: "Thank you, God, for giving me this pleasure. I know it must be from You."

And if your mind can't buy those lies or can't find another lie to buy, it will just shut down.

6. Rational thought ceases and emotion rules.

My guess is that David created some misguided justification through a process similar to the above five steps. Or perhaps his mind shut down and wouldn't let him think about what he was doing. Somehow I doubt that he talked himself into believing that Bathsheba was a gift from God. He knew better than that.

Don't you think?

But let's change the focus from David to you. Think of some sin you can't believe you did. Does the process described in the paragraphs above sound familiar? When I describe this in sermons across the globe, I ask, "Besides me, has anyone here ever gone through this process?" I always see people in the audience nodding. Some are actually brave enough to raise their hands.

Perhaps you haven't experienced it just as I described, but I'm sure you've experienced something similar. You can remember all too well times when your flesh defeated your mind.

We're all sinners. There is no doubt about that.

But some of us have difficulty accepting that we are sinners at the outset of our sinfulness. We've all experienced those actions we like to call "slips" or "mistakes" or something that doesn't sound as bad as "sin." We justify our actions by blaming circumstances, the company we kept, or an extenuating cause. We also tell ourselves the lie that the next time we face that temptation, it won't hold nearly the power it held this time because we'll be prepared.

And, of course, we sin again.

Repetitive Sin

The power of the human mind cannot defeat the weakness in us, much less the power of satanic forces. But it can get worse than that. Not only can evil and flesh defeat the mind, they can make it an ally in the sin.

Especially repetitive sin.

You know what I mean by repetitive sin, don't you? Perhaps you sinned and felt terrible because of it. As you fell on your knees before God, you prayed with a breaking heart, "Oh, God! I'm so sorry for what I've done. If somehow you can find it in your heart to forgive me, I promise that I'll never, ever do it again!"

Have you?

I mean, have you repeated a sin that you promised God in prayer that you would never do again?

Welcome to the human race.

Every audience I've asked that question has been filled with people who sadly raise their hands to admit their failures. Most of us know what it feels like to promise we won't sin again, only to find ourselves doing just that. The satanic strategy is brilliant here. As long as we feel personal guilt for the sin, Satan's forces pretty much leave us alone. But the feeling of personal guilt eventually subsides from its initial level of shame and resolve. And when it does, satanic forces love to use our fleshly desires to bring back the memory of the pleasurable aspects of the sin. If we allow ourselves to think about the sin, our minds relive it, feeling a mixture of revulsion (as influenced by the Spirit) and enjoyment (as influenced by the flesh). As we fantasize about the experience, remembering it vividly, either our disgust or our desire grows. If the memory brings more desire than disgust, we soon find ourselves headed back toward temptation.

Because Christians cannot justify going where the temptation is, knowing the likelihood of sinning when they arrive, they lie to themselves. "I'm not going *there*. I'm not going to do *that*." They insistently delude themselves even while they're in the car or on the bike or placing one foot after the other in the direction of the temptation. Still they think, "I'm not really going there. I'm not going to do that again."

Because it is too difficult to actually arrive at the locale while still pretending not to go there, they finally have to shut down all mental processes. They go mentally numb. Of course, when they arrive at their destinations, they sin again. But the decision to sin wasn't made after they arrived. For all practical purposes, they made it when they became mentally numb.

Sometimes Christians are delivered when the numbness doesn't come quickly enough. If they arrive before their minds shut down, they may well turn around and leave. Or stop along the way.

But those occasions only occur when God's Spirit, working through a person's spirit, overcomes the flesh. They don't come through mental self-discipline.

If we allow ourselves to go numb—and stay numb long enough—we will commit the sin.

Addiction to Sin

When we yield to the same temptations over and over again, we gradually become addicted to the sin.

Oh, this doesn't happen at first. We pray again, "God, I'm so sorry. I know I promised you I wouldn't do it again. But this time I mean it. I will not commit that sin again."

Don't think for a moment that Satan sees your remorse and, in a moment of pity and compassion, says to his forces, "You see that? She feels so badly about that sin. Don't tempt her with that one again." Not a chance. If he says anything at all, it is, "See that? Weakness! Let the guilt settle a bit, and then use the memory to tempt her again. Maybe even get a friend to help get her to the right place at the right time."

To do the wrong thing.

The consequence is more than offending God through our repetitive sin. It affects us as well. No one can continue to pray for forgiveness for the same sin over and over again. Sooner or later we quit praying altogether. Feeling that God doesn't want to hear from sinners like us, we simply fade into spiritual lethargy. And in time, our faith, badly eroded by personal guilt, may fail. If that happens, we no longer feel anything from God or about God.

When addiction to sin takes root, the addiction isn't just of flesh. It's also of mind.

For example, repetitive drunkenness not only makes the body dependent on alcohol, it makes the mind dependent on it as well. The mind and the body are so closely connected that your brain continually sends your body commands that never cross your consciousness. You breathe, swallow, or reach to turn a page without having to give conscious orders to your lungs, throat muscles, or arm. As the body becomes addicted to anything—a drug, an action, a habit—the mind begins to crave it as well. When any activity carries with it the potential for mental or emotional addiction, the passions of the sinful nature can so overpower the mind that those addictions take root and eventually control the mind completely. If you think this is an overstatement, read again the passages from Romans 7.

It happens all the time.

Some people become addicted to alcohol. Others to cocaine or heroin. Some to glue. But even more become addicted to power, sex, lying, gossip, jealousy, or that person they believe they can't live without.

It sometimes seems that those mental addictions are more diffi-cult to overcome than physical addictions. At least with drugs a person can be "dried out." Isolation and medical treatments can help. But someone addicted to a person, position, or thing doesn't have those aids, at least not in the same way.

On the day I wrote these words, I dealt by phone with two people in different parts of America who are addicted to illicit lovers. It happens that both are men, but my experience proves that women can become addicted as well. Each holds a leading position in his church. Each has a wife who loves him deeply and is devastated by the infidelity. Each is addicted to a young woman and can't seem to find a way to overcome the addiction.

No, not child molesters.

Adulterers.

With women twenty years younger than themselves.

Don't read the sentences above with indignation. Read them with prayer. Neither man meant to sin. Neither wanted to do evil. Each developed a friendship that gradually came under control of the sinful nature. Each feels that the younger woman in his life ful-fills certain needs that no other person ever has . . . or ever will. Each believes sincerely and completely that he feels total, uncon-ditional love for his illicit lover, and, more importantly, that she is equally in love with him.

What hospital ward can I place them in for thirty days to "dry" them out? What medicine can I give them to counteract the heady sensations of such romantic ecstasy?

Each, without doubt, is addicted, but neither believes he is. Like alcoholics or drug addicts, they believe they only involve themselves in their adulterous relationships because they wish to. They think that if they wanted to, they could walk away.

But they can't. No more than Ned could resist drinking to drunkenness once he sipped the first cocktail in a social setting.

No addiction can ever be defeated by the mind overcoming the power of the flesh. Something more is needed. And that something is the Holy Spirit.

THE SINFULNESS OF THE SPIRIT

You may think that what I wrote in the last chapter indicates that your spirit is always godly, that it's always seeking God. While it is true that your spirit longs for God, it, too, can be contaminated by sin. As Paul wrote, "Let us purify ourselves from everything that contaminates body and spirit."[21]

When Paul wrote, "May your whole spirit, soul and body be kept blameless at the coming of our Lord Jesus Christ,"[22] he, by that very admonition, implied that the spirit can be blamed. That means the spirit can be held accountable for sin.

Sin touches each part of us. Sin springs from each part of us. Good things are born of the spirit. Selfish things are born of the flesh. As the flesh elicits cooperation from the mind and the spirit, we sin in totality.

Please don't get confused here. I'm not like the Gnostics John addressed in 1 John. I don't believe that the flesh can sin as the spirit remains above it, staying somehow clean and untouched. People who believe that, believe they don't sin. John was right to say, "If we claim to be without sin, we deceive ourselves and the truth is not in us."[23]

I'm saying that the flesh is the perpetrator that enlists the mind and the spirit to sin. The mind may not want to sin initially. Like Paul, we may say, "I . . . in my mind am a slave to God's law, but in the sinful nature a slave to the law of sin."[24] But none of us—not you, not me, not Ned—can commit a sin without the involvement of the mind, body, and spirit. Just as we cannot reach for an object without the mind directing the arm, wrist, and fingers, so we cannot do *anything* without the express cooperation of the mind. And any act, if sinful, dirties us completely—even spiritually. The whole of a person—body, mind, and spirit—commits the sin. If we commit the sin, our spirit is involved whether it wants to be or not. It can't "sit out" the sin. As an integral part of our trinary nature, it is a joint participant.

Do you grasp the importance of this?

I cannot stop myself from sinning by the power of my mind, no matter how much I discipline it or how strong my will.

Neither can I stop myself from sinning by the power of my spirit, no matter how close it is to God or how much I commune with Him through prayer and Bible study.

My flesh can, and will, overpower both of them.

So, is there no hope?

If you stop there, no, there isn't.

But if you read the rest of what God says about victory over sin and guilt, there is great hope. Wonderful hope. Victorious hope.

In this chapter you've seen why we sin, even when we don't want to. And when we sin, guilt overwhelms us and our hearts cry our for peace. But sometimes we try to take matters into our own hands and write our own prescription for the cure. In the next chapter, we'll examine some of the things we humans do in an effort to dull the ache of guilt.

Repressed guilt is not removed guilt. It's just guilt hiding under deception.

❧

For it is by grace you have been saved, through faith—and this not from yourselves, it is the gift of God.

Ephesians 2:8

CHAPTER 5

What Can I Do to Stop Feeling Guilty?

Watching Perry lumber across the foyer, I momentarily lost control of my Sunday morning ministerial dignity and let out a guffaw. No, not because of his looks. Actually he's a rather comfortable-looking gentleman, as relaxed and inviting as a well-broken-in recliner. When he heard my laughter, he smiled his slow, friendly smile and let loose a twinkle in his eye that immediately put me on humor guard. I never know what to expect from Perry Greer, a gentle retiree who looks about as dangerous as an old hound sleeping in the corner. But I knew better than to let that fool me. One Sunday a few months ago, he grinned all the way to his pew, head up, gait slow and regal, and then sat there acting innocent.

His head was shaved as clean as a cue ball.

Just as white and glossy too.

No one said a word to him—nobody knew what to say—but everyone stared. Well, almost everyone. His wife sat three rows away and resolutely refused to look his direction. I don't know how she did it; my eyes were drawn to him like a tongue exploring the hole left by a recently vacated tooth. I couldn't help but look. I watched him throughout the entire sermon.

And I was preaching.

So I didn't know what to expect when Perry approached me after my sermon on this Sunday. As he reached me, he spoke, wrapping his warm Southern drawl around his words. "You know that thing you were preaching about this mornin'? About guilt? Couple years ago I was buying a Sunday paper. Dropped my dollar and a quarter into the machine, and while I was gettin' my paper I noticed this man who'd walked up behind me. Just being nice, you know, I held the door open while he took a paper.

"Well sir, he just up and walked away. Didn't put any money in the machine at all. It made me feel guilty. I'd helped him steal a paper! It was me that held the door open.

"I worried about that all week. It really bothered me. So next Sunday I put it back."

"You did what?" I asked.

"I went back to that same box, put my dollar and a quarter in, got my newspaper, and put the newspaper I bought the Sunday before back in."

I held my composure for all of two seconds and then collapsed in a laughter meltdown. I could just see some guy coming along, dropping his money into the slot, retrieving a newspaper, and then, halfway home, realizing he had last Sunday's edition! It would cost him another dollar and a quarter just to get the right one. My "Three Stooges" gene—the one that most men inherit but most women don't—kicked into overdrive, dumping my Christian compassion right out the door. Slapstick ruled over spirituality.

"Stop!" I gasped, "You're killing me. That's just too funny. How do you think these things up?"

"I'm not makin' it up." Perry frowned. "I really did it. I put it back. I didn't want to go to hell for a dollar and a quarter."

He was serious.

Perry Greer irrationally feared losing his soul over a Sunday newspaper, so he did what he could to make it right. But the frown on his face evidenced the doubt that his restitution was enough. That didn't surprise me. Restitution never is.

You may read Perry's story and ask, "You think I relate to someone who inadvertently helped some guy steal a newspaper? I wish what I feel guilty about was as inconsequential as that. I'd happily spend some loose change to reload a newspaper box if that would make my fear, shame, and guilt go away. As a matter of fact, if you can just tell me what to do to feel better, I'll do it—whatever it takes."

If you feel this way, I say the same thing to you that I said about Perry's returning the newspaper. Restitution is a nice gesture, but it never undoes the act. Nor does it have to in order for God to forgive you.

Don't worry, Perry, my point isn't about your returning the newspaper. You're a wonderful, gentle man who tried to make up for a sin you didn't even commit. My point is that neither contrition, restitution, nor any other act has the power to undo the wrong we do.

We can't remove "small" sins.

We can't remove "major" sins.

We can never conquer sin or guilt through our own will power. Only God can do that. No human ever will.

You may be thinking, "You missed it here, Joe. I have conquered my own sin and extinguished my own guilt."

I ask you, "Are you sure? Did you actually remove the sin and guilt, or did you merely *repress* it?" You see, repressed guilt may be so blocked that it doesn't regularly reach the conscience. But don't be fooled. It's still there.

Anyone can repress guilt. Just drink enough alcohol, take enough pills, lie to yourself long enough, or get some misguided therapist to lie to you until you believe the lies. Reframe. Pretend. Force yourself into a busied state that doesn't allow reflection. There are lots of tools. Just choose one.

But the personal guilt will still be there, and the temptation will eventually return, coming at the right place and the right time to catch you at your weakest. The feelings of guilt will come again too. And the guilt from all your wrongs—whether you consider them "minor" or "major"—will band together to become a formidable force festering just beneath the surface—sabotaging the body and waiting to ambush the mind. Repressed personal guilt is not removed guilt. It's just guilt hiding under deception.

Interestingly, many Christian people practice a form of repression when they try to deal with their sins or guilt through their own actions. They may well be good actions, even biblical actions. But, too often, they are misunderstood actions: things God wants us to do but never wanted us to think of as solutions to our guilt problems.

What kinds of things?

Let's look at a few.

RESTITUTION

We Christians teach people they should make restitution for their wrongs, and rightly so. If you steal money, give it back. If you lie, confess to the people you lied to and then tell the truth.

If you steal a newspaper, put it back.

Next week.

Just kidding!

Put it back the same day you steal it.

Restitution is a biblical concept. Just read the first fifteen verses of Exodus 22 and you'll see that God made restitution a part of the Law of Moses. But He doesn't say to just give back what you stole; He says to give more. The person hurt by the theft gains in the process of your restitution. If Perry had read that chapter, he'd have put four newspapers back. That's what Exodus 22 demands— fourfold restitution.

But restitution becomes a problem when people think it is the solution to their guilt problem: Just undo what you did and everything will be fine. I heard one preacher say, "Steal a donkey; give it back. Steal a cow; give it back. Take another man's wife; give her back." (Yes, he actually said it just that way. I don't think he realized that he equated a wife with livestock.)

Stealing, adultery, divorce, remarriage—just fix everything by restoring all to what it was before. Of course, if we want to be more scriptural in our application, we would return four donkeys, four cows, and *four wives*.

Now you have to admit, that would be interesting.

But restitution doesn't "fix" anything. I don't believe God meant us to believe that it would. Restitution is an act of remorse on the part of the sinner that demonstrates a desire to undo a wrong. It's a godly act. It is good for the sinner, and it is good for the one against whom the sin was committed. When restitution can logically be done, it should be done. But there definitely are times when restitution is impossible.

You can't give back a life ripped from a body by murder. And you can't give back a wife, not if she's now married to someone else.[1] The fact is, you can never give enough to remove the shame of sin—any sin.

Restitution helps the intellect: "I've done what I can. There is no more I can reasonably do." But it doesn't always help the emotions, and it most certainly doesn't help the spirit. The damaged relationship with God isn't cured by giving back more than was taken. The human penalty of sin requires temporal payback when possible. But sin reaches beyond the human and the temporal. Our sins are also against God, and for that reason they carry spiritual dimensions and spiritual consequences. God says that our sin—any sin—earns us death.[2] Only He can abrogate the guilt, and only He can remove the death penalty.

Consider this in human terms: I could not commute a duly processed and declared death sentence against me by any act of restitution. No human can. Would society have allowed Ted Bundy, notorious serial killer, to avoid execution and leave jail if he could have found some way to make restitution to his victims' families?

No.

The victims' families didn't declare him guilty and condemn him to death. The state of Florida did. No restitution to those families could abrogate the demands of the law. Only that government whose laws he violated could change his death sentence or give him reprieve.

So it is with the law of God. If I sin against you, I can offer you restitution. You may accept it and forgive me. Your forgiveness may rid me of feeling personal guilt about the sin. But I still must face God. I broke His law, and so I must face His penalty. My sin and my legal guilt can only be removed by Him.

Not by you.

Not by me.

Only by Him.

And the restoration of an unhindered relationship between His Spirit and my spirit can only take place when He removes my guilt.

Not you.

Not me.

Just Him.

Unless I know His grace, my personal guilt will return with the next temptation. Never can I make enough restitution to make myself believe that I've "paid back" all I owe.

So, restitution is godly, meaningful, and helps mend relationships between sinners and those they sinned against. It even gives some peace of mind to sinners. It may even make us think twice when the temptation comes again—having to give back four sheep for stealing one is quite a deterrent.

But could thieves be tempted to steal again, even if they'd made restitution for the last theft? Could child abusers be tempted to abuse again, even if they had made restitution to society by serving a prison sentence for the last crime? Restitution may be a deterrent, but it is not a roadblock.

Restitution doesn't mean a person has conquered sin or, necessarily, that the person has been legally forgiven. Restitution is useless when made by a person who isn't saved. If that happens, the person isn't healed but deceived. Don't misunderstand, I'm not saying that someone making restitution hasn't already been forgiven; I'm saying that restitution will never gain forgiveness.

Something more than restitution is needed to remove legal guilt. Only God's grace can do that.

CONTRITION

You may be thinking, "Would feeling really bad about what I've done keep me from sinning and remove legal and personal guilt? After all, God says He wants a contrite heart, doesn't He?"

Yes, that's right, God does want contrite hearts. The psalmist wrote, "The Lord is close to the brokenhearted and saves those who are crushed in spirit."[3] God makes it extremely clear that the path to Him cannot be traveled by the proud, the spiritually arrogant, or those who think themselves above sin.

And healing of sin often requires mourning the sin. But contrition or mourning is only a step toward spiritual healing. It is not the healing itself. Feeling bad enough to go to the doctor isn't the same as being in the office and receiving the injection that will make you well. The pain drove you there, but the pain didn't heal you.

In the same way, contrition can drive people to find the healing power of God. But it doesn't always. Sometimes it so debilitates us that we cannot do anything—not even seek the Great Physician. The very thing that should drive us to seek help makes us shut down and do nothing.

I vividly remember attending the funeral of a young husband and father who died needlessly because he wouldn't seek medical help. His disease caused him great pain and weakness, so much that he couldn't work. He lay in his bed, telling his wife how he hurt and how he longed to be well again. She begged him to call a doctor, but he ignored her. She asked if she could call an ambulance, but he insisted he would be all right in a day or two. Then he moaned again about how bad he felt. He remained in his sickbed, lamenting his disease, until he died.

I've seen people do the same thing spiritually. They feel contrition. No one could feel more guilt or shame or degradation than they do. But rather than seek God's healing power, they avoid Him. Perhaps they're afraid of His reaction. It could be that they think they aren't worthy to receive His healing. Or maybe they think they aren't finished with the sin yet. "I want God to make this guilt and shame go away . . . but I can't promise Him I won't do the very same thing tomorrow."

How can a person feel contrition, guilt, and sinful desire at the same time?

Because being sorry you sinned doesn't mean you won't sin again or that the temptation no longer holds any attraction for you. Satanic forces have a way of waiting for sorrow to subside. Then they hit with just the right temptation to make you forget your shame and join their game.

Contrite, brokenhearted people can commit their sin again . . . and feel the same overwhelming sorrow again. They may even feel worse than before. But contrition can't overcome personal guilt, and contrition can't heal.

Amazing, isn't it? The very thing God wants—a broken heart— and the contrite person still feels guilty. Why?

Because contrition is only a part of the path to healing; it is not the destination.

SPIRITUAL BALANCING

Sometimes when we can't stop our sin or remove our guilt by restitution or contrition, we try a sort of spiritual balancing. We try to be good enough to make up for how bad we've been. Of course, such efforts are doomed to failure. My friend Jimmy Allen, to whom this book is dedicated, says, "There are two things true of a person trying to work his way to heaven. First, he's very busy. Second, he's very frustrated."

Having tried to work my way to heaven, and having helped many others who have tried, I wholeheartedly agree. We can't be busy enough to live above temptation, and we can't do enough good to make God forget the evil we've done. Good works won't save us.[4] Nor will they take us past the personal guilt we feel deep within us.

Several years ago I counseled a young Christian lady who struggled with sin. In the six months I tried to help her, she slept with a dozen men. She tried to live the Christian life, but she was tormented by an inner demon neither of us understood at the time. Guilt hounded her every waking minute, torturing her and luring her toward suicide. Yet, even while carrying that unbearable load, she'd sin with a new partner within days of the last degrading encounter. Every degrading encounter heaped greater personal guilt on her. But instead of her awareness driving her toward God's healing, her overwhelming sense of hopelessness drove her even deeper into sin. She didn't know how to win the battle and neither did I—her spiritual helper. (I was twenty-two at the time—young enough to think I had all the answers and old enough to be in a helping position as a minister. Quite a dangerous combination.)

Since my counseling didn't help her, she did the only thing she knew to do. She threw herself completely into church work—any activity, every event, whatever anyone needed. I sat in the audience once as a preacher held her up as a positive example for the whole church, telling us if we could be just a fraction as involved as she, the church would soar in its service to God. I never took my eyes from her as he lavishly praised her. Sitting across the aisle from her and one row back, I could see her profile but not her eyes. I could see she was smiling modestly—what else could she do? But as I watched, I saw something that seemed to escape everyone else's notice. As the minister spoke, she slowly, sadly shook her head from side to side. I knew that slight gesture of "no" wasn't modesty. She heard his praise for her acts of balance and came into confrontation with the heartbreaking truth. Her service was empty. No amount of giving, sharing, teaching, working, supporting, or leading can balance out fornication.

Twelve guys in six months.

What could she do to remove that from the books? What Christian involvement could keep her from the next rendezvous? How much activity in the Kingdom would free her conscience?

Maybe you've encountered the same attitude, though on a lesser scale. Perhaps a man teaches a Bible class because he feels guilty about his language at work. But teaching the class doesn't clean up his communication nor does it make him feel any less guilty about it. Perhaps a woman sings in the choral group because she feels guilty about not reading her Bible or praying except during church services. Sadly she finds that neither Bible study nor prayer increases, and the guilt continues to gently tug at her. Yet another Christian might serve as a deacon because he feels guilty about being a selfish husband and an always-absent dad. But neither the church title nor the responsibilities that come with it change a thing about his actions or his guilt.

It doesn't work.

It can't work.

Balancing, by its very nature, puts us in the place of God. Guilt-caged balancers inadvertently put themselves in God's place as they doubt God's forgiveness and healing. Deceived balancers believe they are so obedient or so full of good works they don't need God. The guilt-caged doubts; the deceived supplants. But neither will achieve the goal of making up for sin by doing good deeds or offering enough obedience.

Not only does balancing not work; it becomes a vicious cycle. Since they can't be good enough to make up for what they've done in the past, much less for the things they continue to do, they try to do still more. Their "acts of Christian service" increase as their sin or guilt increases.

God created us to do good works for Him, not for ourselves.[5] But in trying to balance our lives, we do good deeds for ourselves. In these cases, our actions aren't gifts to God; they're misguided bribes.

Good works will never stop us from sinning or save us from

judgment. Only God's grace can do that. And good works won't free our hearts from the personal guilt that torments us.

CONFESSION

What, then, can stop sin and remove guilt? Will confession do it? Some Christians think so. For them, confession is almost mystical in its power to stop sin and remove guilt. But the way they use it won't work.

It's absolutely true that confession is a part of the healing process. God commands it. He expects it.[6] In the last chapter of this book, we will discuss it in depth. But confession, standing alone, also is inadequate to remove sin or guilt. Even personal guilt.

I remember clearly one particular night during the three years I lived apart from my family and my God. I almost always went to church—habits die hard—but my spiritual life displayed few other signs of life. I was at church that night. Because of overpowering guilt for something I had done that several people had discovered, I confessed before the whole church at the evening service. I told them and God that I was terribly sorry for what I had done. And I meant it. I was terribly sorry. But before I reached my apartment that night, through no planning or actions of my own, I found myself at the right place at the right time.

And I did the wrong thing.

A really wrong thing.

Neither genuine contrition nor confession stopped me from sinning. And they certainly didn't cure me of my guilt. I felt worse than I did before I confessed. I stood just as much in need of healing, if not more so, as I had before I confessed. I was a guilt-caged Christian, so immobilized by my guilt that I could not find God's power to conquer the sin or find the peace of personal healing.

Don't pity me for that time in my life. We are all the same. None of us can stop ourselves from sinning or heal ourselves of guilt no matter what restitution we attempt or accomplish, no matter how bad we feel, no matter how many good things we do, no matter how much we tell people—or God—what sinners we are or how sorry we are. We will never stop ourselves from sinning, and we will never be able to remove our guilt. Certainly not legal guilt. Sadly, not even personal guilt.

Restitution, contrition, balancing, and confession—all godly acts. Some are part of the healing process. But not one of them can heal us of sin or guilt. They can't even accomplish that when they're all bound together. Only God can heal.

Only He can stop the sin and cure the guilt.

If you've been trying to remove your guilt by any of these methods—or by some method not mentioned here—stop. Oh, no, don't quit the good deeds. Just stop expecting anything you do to accomplish what only He can do. Leave your frustration behind by allowing God to heal you of sin and guilt.

How?

I think it's time we answered that.

We start in the next chapter.

PART TWO

ACCEPTING GOD'S FORGIVENESS

❧

The more you believe that God
has completely forgiven everything
you've ever done, the less power
your flesh will have.

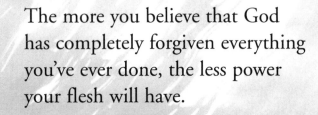

*As far as the east is from the west, so far has
he removed our transgressions from us.*

Psalm 103:12

6

Believe What God Tells You about You

"Am I late?"

I smiled to see him. Bobby served as one of our deacons and was, by my estimation, one of the best "good old boys" in our small Southern town. I was all of twenty-two years old, serving a small church in my first full-time ministry while completing my degree at a Bible college ninety miles away. He'd called to make an appointment with me so I could help him with a spiritual matter. I admit I felt rather important to be considered worthy of giving spiritual counsel to an older and presumably wiser man. But I also feared that I would most certainly demonstrate my spiritual immaturity by having no clue as to what to tell him.

"C'mon in. Have a seat."

"Thanks. Believe I will." He smiled back at me as he eased his lanky frame into the chair across from my desk.

I moved around to the chair next to him and sat there smiling, wondering what I was supposed to say next. He smiled back, not saying anything either. Drawing a blank on what the niceties of counseling might be and thinking we might sit there grinning for hours, I figured we should just get right to it. "What can I do for you?"

Immediately Bobby's expression changed. His good-old-boy smile melted into a creased brow, troubled eyes, and downturned lips.

"Sin," he said softly. "I've been dealing with guilt for fifteen years over a willful sin. I've prayed and studied and prayed some more. I've told my wife, and she's prayed about it too. I just can't get past this thing, and it's killing me."

Then he uttered the words that I didn't want to hear, words that terrified my young, inexperienced mind. "I came for you to fix it."

I was afraid to ask but knew I had to. "What are you doing, Bobby? What is your willful sin?"

"Oh, no, you don't understand. I'm not doing it now. It's something I did fifteen years ago when I was in the army stationed in Germany. I . . . uh . . . I . . ."

As he searched for the courage to tell me, my mind raced through possibilities, bracing myself not to react when he told me his heinous crime. Adultery? Theft? Drunkenness? Or maybe all of those combined? My goodness, could it be murder? I tensed, took a deep breath, and resolved that whatever it was I would act as if I heard it every day.

"I . . . well, I didn't go to church hardly at all the whole time I was there. Almost a year."

He paused, head down. I prompted him for the sordid part of the story. "Okay, Bobby, you didn't go to church like you should. And . . ?"

"And what?" he responded.

"And what did you do while you were in Germany that you feel so guilty about fifteen years later?"

He stared at me as if I were the dumbest preacher he'd ever met—like maybe he should find one who had actually graduated.

"I told you what I did! For almost a whole year I didn't go to church. That's a willful sin, you know. I grew up in a home where I was taught right and lived right and went to church every Sunday without fail. While I was in Germany, my wife went to church every Sunday like she should. My wife, my in-laws, my mama—everybody thought I was doing right, and there I was, not going to church hardly at all. I let 'em down. I let God down. Man, I was just no good."

I've already told you that I was the greenest of the green, but I just couldn't believe this man carried so much guilt over a year of lapsed church attendance. So I determinedly pursued his "real" sin.

"What else, Bobby? Was it gambling? Drinking? Maybe a woman?"

"You deaf, boy? I told you what I did and how bad I feel about it. I've prayed for fifteen years God would forgive me, but I feel just as guilty as I did back then. Nothing helps. I go to church. I give 10 percent of my income to God. I teach Bible class. And I feel rotten inside."

He paused, then demanded, "You gonna fix it or not?"

Sometimes God has to intervene so we don't totally ruin things through our own stupidity. I'm sure that's what He did that day. I was too young and too naive to understand that personal guilt doesn't have to spring from "major" sins. Anything we do that violates God can eat us alive. Bobby was the classic example of what I would later designate a guilt-caged Christian.

I opened my mouth to respond and found myself saying something wiser than I was. God indeed answered the prayer for wisdom I'd prayed before Bobby arrived. Rather than quote Scripture to a man who likely knew more Scripture than I did, I replied with a story—a parable, if you will.

"Bobby, let's put this into perspective. Suppose one morning before you leave for work you tell your son, Jeff, to feed those hunting dogs you keep in that pen next to your shed. When you get home late that afternoon you see the dogs acting sort of wilted and walk out to check on them. You know a lot about dogs, and it takes you only a minute or so to figure out they're hungry. They haven't been fed.

"Naturally, you yell for Jeff to come outside. You ask him if he fed those dogs. Jeff says, 'Naw, Daddy, I forgot. I got so busy tryin' to get off to school this mornin' and then playin' when I got home that I forgot. I'm sorry. Please forgive me, Daddy; I'll feed 'em right now.'

"You'd probably get on to him a little bit, watch him feed the dogs, tell him everything's all right, and then go on about your business. By the next day you wouldn't even be thinking about it anymore. Is that right, Bobby?"

It was clear he couldn't see the relevance of my story to his situation, but he humored me anyway. "Yeah. That'd be about the way it would happen."

"Now, suppose the next day you get home from work and all the kids are in that big front yard of yours playing football. All the kids, that is, except Jeff. He's sitting under a tree moping, looking real sad. You walk over and ask, 'Son, what's the matter?' Jeff hangs his head and says, 'Dad, I feel so guilty about not feeding them dogs yesterday.' I think I know what you'd say, Bobby. You'd say, 'Son, that's over and done with. I know you're sorry about not doin' what I told you to do. You told me that yesterday, and I told you I forgave you. Forget about it, boy.'"

He nodded his head. Yes, that's what he'd say.

"Bobby, Jeff's only ten years old now. Suppose when he's eighteen and graduating from high school, he walks across the stage to receive his diploma, stops, looks at you in the audience, and tearfully says, 'Dad, I feel so bad about them dogs. Can you ever forgive me?' That'd make you feel pretty bad, wouldn't it, Bobby?"

120

He didn't answer. He was thinking.

"Now, Bobby, let's move it ahead to when Jeff's twenty-five years old. He lives in another city but is coming home for Thanksgiving with his wife and son—your grandbaby. You haven't seen him in six months, can't wait to be with him. But as he walks through the door of your house, he hangs his head, unable to look you in the eye. He says, 'Daddy, remember those dogs? I just can't get over what I did to them. You told me to feed them, and I ignored your will for my pleasure. Dad, can you ever forgive me?'

"That's fifteen years after the 'sin.' I know it's sort of a foolish illustration, but if Jeff did that, Bobby, how would you feel? You, his father who had long since forgiven him. What would you think if he felt bad about a sin you forgave fifteen years earlier?"

With red-rimmed eyes, Bobby said, "I'd think that he didn't believe his daddy."

"Ah, Bobby. That's it. You don't believe your Father. You think maybe He's just as hurt because you don't believe He's forgiven you as you'd be if Jeff didn't believe you'd forgiven him."

Bobby was silent. "I can't fix it, Bobby. But you will begin to realize spiritual healing just as soon as you *believe what God tells you about you.*"

Most Christians who struggle with guilt have the same problem as Bobby. They simply don't believe their Father.

THE POWER OF GOD . . . THE POWER OF FAITH

Your sin may seem "bigger" than Bobby's. Maybe yours is adultery, drunkenness, or murder. It makes no difference. The size of the guilt is irrelevant.

Sometimes the sin carries greater consequence in the eyes of society, especially church society. Sometimes other people can't fathom why the sinner feels so guilty, when by their standards, the sinner hardly did anything wrong at all. But from your own life you know that the burden of guilt is personal, quite independent from what people tell you you should feel.

We're all in a wretched state and utterly unable to rescue ourselves, no matter how "big" or "little" our sin. We can say with the apostle Paul, "What a wretched man I am! Who will rescue me from this body of death?"[1] You know why he called it the "body of death," don't you? Because it so easily yields to the passions of the flesh—to sin and to sin again. But Paul immediately followed his sad lament with a shout of thanksgiving: "Thanks be to God—through Jesus Christ our Lord!"[2]

Victory over sin is ours!

Victory over guilt is ours!

But the victory is not really "ours."

It is won by a powerful warrior. His name is Jesus.

You know that God forgives. But He does so much more. He gives us victory over ourselves. He conquers our flesh, our shameful memories, our guilt, and our pain. Mine. Yours. Everyone's. But we must *believe* it is for us. That is where the healing lies.

When Jesus removes our guilt, he stops the power of sin in us, and healing begins.

Earlier I wrote that we cannot stop sinning by the power of our minds or our spirits. Let's recast those thoughts with a slight change of emphasis.

- You cannot stop yourself from sinning or from feeling guilt by the power of your mind, no matter how much you discipline you mind or how strong your will.
- You cannot stop yourself from sinning or from feeling guilt by the power of your spirit, no matter how close you are to God or how much you commune with Him through prayer and Bible study.

Do you see the power of those truths? Do you see how hopeless we are within ourselves? We are helpless to stop ourselves from sinning, and we are just as helpless to stop ourselves from feeling personal guilt. Victory over sin, legal guilt, and personal guilt *must* come through Jesus.

But the efficacy of what Jesus does is directly dependent on our *acceptance* of what Jesus did for us. Forgiveness, healing, and renewal are matters of faith in the work of God. Nothing else. The first and most important step to being healed from sin and guilt is believing what God tells us about us.

"YOUR SINS ARE FORGIVEN"

I guess we could argue over whether Jesus does the forgiving or whether He just made it possible for God to forgive. We know from Sunday school that God loved us enough to give Jesus to die for us.[3] The Father's love sent Him, and the Father's love kept Him on task when fear weakened Him.[4] So, who can say God doesn't forgive? Certainly He does.

But it is Jesus who will sit on the judgment throne on the final day as we receive what is due us "for the things done while in the body, whether good or bad."[5] Therefore, it is the Son, not the Father, who will look each saint in the eye and say, "I forgive. Enter."

No, I don't know that He will say those exact words.

Maybe He'll elaborate more.

Or maybe He'll just smile and gesture for us to come in.

It wouldn't surprise me at all if He hugged each of us warmly and slowly. We won't care how long we wait in line.

Whatever He says or does, I think judgment day will be a glorious occasion for Him as He sees the fruit of His mission. Don't you?

Jesus came to this earth with the express purpose of saving us.[6] He doesn't want any of us to be lost.[7] He knew that we deserve death because of our sin, but He chose to take upon Himself the death we earned.[8]

You can choose to believe what Jesus says about you and let Him pay for your sins, or you can choose to handle your sin and salvation yourself. But if you choose to go it alone, the salvation you seek will never be realized. If you allow Him to do it all, you will know the peace and healing that comes from believing His words of forgiveness.

"YOUR GUILT IS REMOVED"

I don't know a better way to say this than in the words of David: "As far as the east is from the west, so far has he removed our transgression from us."[9] Measure that and tell me how far away He casts our forgiven sins from us. When we, like David, beg of God, "Wash away my iniquity and cleanse me from my sin," we can be assured that His cleansing does make us "whiter than snow."[10] God has said that our guilt has been removed; He has said we are clean. It is up to us to believe what He says about us.

No Eternal Consequences

When we surrender in faith to Jesus, we no longer have any legal guilt before God.

None.

When He wipes a slate clean, there are no erasure marks. The sin is gone; the guilt is gone. The record of the crimes no longer exist—no matter what human record may be kept.

All my life I've heard illustrations from preachers trying to convince people not to sin. I remember one illustration well. "A father hammered a nail into a fence post every time his son disobeyed. When the boy did some good deed of obedience, the father removed a nail. One day the dad found the lad sitting by the post crying. Frustrated, the dad asked, 'What's the matter, boy? There aren't any nails in there now.' The boy sobbed, 'I know. But look at all those holes!'"

With the conclusion of this illustration, the preacher bent low over the pulpit and solemnly intoned, "That's what sin does. God may forgive you for your disobedience, but you live with the consequences forever." That's really what he said. I'm not exaggerating. I know—because I was the preacher.

That illustration has at least two theological errors. First, it implies that God removes sin when we balance it with some good act. Second, it tells folks that the "hole"—the consequence of our sin—is there for eternity.

Hogwash.

Or, if you prefer the King James Version, hogwasheth.

It is true that certain types of sin leave an imprint on the human body (like AIDS) or on the human memory, but there are no eternal consequences for forgiven sin. There are no holes to fill. None.

Complete Spiritual Renewal

When Jesus removes our guilt, He sees us as innocent as if we had just been born. As a matter of fact, Jesus told us that if we want to come to Him, we "must be born again."[11] We start new, as if beginning for the first time—not by figuring some way back into our mother's womb so we can try life again from scratch, but by undergoing a complete spiritual renewal from God.

Since God considers us completely new, neither He, Jesus, nor the Holy Spirit will ever bring up the forgiven sin again. Not even on Judgment Day. When God forgives, the sin is totally annihilated. It doesn't exist in you. It doesn't exist in heaven. Guilt is gone.

It can only exist in your memory.

And it will only exist there if you choose to believe it is still there.

Nothing to Fear

When Peter fell at Jesus' knees crying, "Go away from me, Lord; I am a sinful man!"[12] did Jesus go? Or did He say, "You better grovel, you filthy rag. Show me how insignificant a worm you are"? Do you remember reading that Jesus exhorted, "I'll forgive you, but don't you ever forget what you are, you worthless good-for-nothing"? No. He didn't say any of those things. Instead, when in sudden awareness of his sinfulness before a perfect God, Peter begged Him to leave, Jesus replied, *"Don't be afraid."[13]*

Even the most sinful person, when forgiven by Jesus, has nothing to fear. Not Peter. Not a murderer. Not an adulterer. Not a child abuser. Not a liar, a thief, or a glutton. Not me. Not you.

He says we are to believe Him.

Him.

Not our doubts. Not our fears. Not anyone or anything else.

Just Him.

Just like Bobby wanted Jeff to believe him.

And it really is that simple. When we accept (believe, trust) the forgiveness of God, God uses our faith to defeat personal guilt.

You can bury your guilt, but only God can destroy it.

He kills it in the legal annals of heaven.

He kills it in our hearts, minds, and spirits. He simply asks us to believe that it is so.

You may be thinking, "Surely, if it were that easy I would have done it by now." I know it's hard to believe—harder for some than for others. But it's true. The way to be healed is to believe what God tells you about His forgiveness of you.

"YOUR OLD SELF IS CRUCIFIED"

One reason that some find this foundational truth so difficult to believe is that they know they still struggle with the flesh and have not found complete victory over it. They still want to sin, and they still commit sin. Does this describe you? Then don't quit here. Everything I said still applies, even to us struggling sinner-saints.

How?

Well, again, it may be hard to accept, but the first step to overcoming flesh is believing God's power over it. God can conquer it. But we must accept God's power over it.

Let's look at what God said through the apostle Paul in Romans 6: "All of us who were baptized into Christ Jesus were baptized into his death. . . . For we know that our old self was crucified with him so that the body of sin might be done away with, that we should no longer be slaves to sin—because anyone who has died has been freed from sin."[14]

Rendered Powerless

In the passage above, Paul referenced the crucifixion of Jesus, then he stated that our "body of sin" (flesh) might be "done away with" when the "old self" (what we have been and done) is crucified with Jesus. The footnote in the New International Version gives "rendered powerless" as an alternate translation to "done away with." When a person is "baptized into Christ Jesus," the sinful nature is rendered powerless. The flesh loses its power to lead the mind and body to sin.

Paul did not say that the sinful nature is dead and gone. He didn't mean we actually become like dead men who no longer have use of their five senses—no longer able to see, hear, smell, touch, or taste sin. The part of us that wants to sin doesn't cease to exist. All Christians who struggle with temptation know that. What ceases to exist when we come to Jesus is our "old self," the person we were before coming into union with Christ. He said that our past is crucified. Nothing that we have been or done exists any longer. "If anyone is in Christ, he is a new creation; the old has gone, the new has come!"[15]

When I actually *believe* that everything about me that was sinful has been killed, something changes inside. Now, when my flesh responds to a temptation, my spirit rises up, armed with the power that comes from feeling guiltless. Knowing that I am sinless changes my perceptions, my desires, and my actions. Seeing myself as new, holy, and clean makes me want to live in harmony with the new me who now has harmony with God. Therefore, the flesh is "rendered powerless." The peace with God and self that results from believing I am guiltless dramatically weakens the power of the flesh to lead me into sin.

The most vivid illustration I can give of this power over flesh may seem foolish to you, but it was a revelation to me. A few years ago, I dreamed one night that I was again involved in the sin that nearly destroyed my family and me. The dream was vivid, one of those where you think you must be awake because you see things so clearly and feel them so intensely.

Throughout the dream I struggled with a mixture of desire and remorse. I wanted to do right, but I also wanted to possess that which tempted me so. Like the illusion inherent in most dreams, not everything was in order, but somehow I knew I'd already sinned and was facing the possibility of continuing the sin if I wished.

And that's exactly what I did. I watched it unfold on the screen of my mind. Horrified and mesmerized, but unable to resist the opportunity.

When, finally, by the grace of God, I awoke, it took several moments to realize I was in my own bed and that none of it had happened. As soon as I was sure of that, I sailed from the desire to surrender to my flesh to a great victory over it. I was clean! I hadn't done those things! Emotions flooding through me from that awareness pushed me to a pinnacle of spiritual strength. If the very temptation that had moments before so seduced me in my sleep could have somehow bodily walked through my bedroom door, I would have laughed at its foolishness.

I was innocent, and I was going to stay innocent!

I no longer wanted to be—or would surrender to be—what I had been before. All my sins were gone and I had no desire to have them back. Jesus took them from me and I intended to let Him keep them.

When believers come into contact with the crucifixion of Jesus, all their sins transfer from them to Him. All their past—no matter how sordid or shameful—goes onto the "scapegoat,"[16] so that for them all things are new.

They, quite simply, are not the people they were. They aren't the people who sinned fifteen years ago, fifteen months ago, fifteen days ago, or fifteen minutes ago. They are completely new. Just as Jesus resurrected from His burial with a new and different body,[17] so we resurrect from our burial with Him as new and different people.[18]

To find peace and healing, we must believe that.

Count Yourself Dead to Sin

The same faith that led us to God should also lead us to believe on the power of God over all parts of our lives—including our flesh. Paul said that: "Now if we died with Christ, we believe that we will also live with him."[19] See the part faith plays? "We *believe*," he said. Then he wrote, "In the same way, count yourselves dead to sin but alive to God in Christ Jesus."[20]

"Count"?

That means accept it as being true. Know that the faith that led you to believe in Jesus should also lead you to accept as true the fact that your sinful past is completely obliterated in Him. The King James Version says "reckon ye yourselves," the New American Standard translates it as "consider yourselves," and the New International Version offers "count yourselves." They all mean the same thing. Believe it to be true and act accordingly.

John Stott, in his book *Men Made New*, says this about "reckoning":

> Now "reckoning" is not make-believe. It is not screwing up our faith to believe something we do not believe. We are not to pretend that our old nature [flesh, sinful nature] has died when we know perfectly well that it has not. We are rather to realize that our old self—that is our former self—did die, thus paying the penalty of its sins and putting an end to its career. . . . I find it helpful to think in these terms. Our biography is written in two volumes. Volume one is the story of the old man, the old self, of me before my conversion. Volume two is the story of the new man, the new self, of me after I was made a new creation in Christ. Volume one of my biography ended with the judicial death of the old self. I was a sinner. I deserved to die. I did die. I received my desserts in my Substitute with whom I have become one. Volume two of my biography opened with my resurrection. My old life having finished, a new life to God has begun. We are simply called to "reckon" this—not to pretend it, but to realize it. It is a fact. And we have to lay hold of it. We have to let our minds play upon these truths. We have to meditate upon them until we grasp them firmly. We have to keep saying to ourselves, "Volume one has closed. You are now living in volume two." It is inconceivable that you should reopen volume one. It is not impossible, but it is inconceivable. . . . So the secret of godly living is in the mind. It is in knowing (verse 6) that our old self was cru-

cified with Christ. It is in knowing (verse 3) that baptism into Christ is baptism into His death and resurrection. It is in reckoning, intellectually realizing (verse 11), that in Christ we have died to sin and we live to God. . . . Our faith and baptism have severed us from the old life, cut us off from it irrevocably, and committed us to the new. Our baptism stands between us and the old life as a door between two rooms, closing the one and opening into the other."[21]

If you still struggle with temptation and sin, don't let that struggle make you doubt your relationship with God; don't doubt His forgiveness. Remember that your flesh is still alive—it will be until that day you leave this body in death. But on those occasions when it rears its ugly head of self-centeredness, don't think that means you are hopeless. The more you believe that God has completely forgiven everything you've ever done—even that stuff you did yesterday—by crucifying the "old man," the less power your flesh will have. Your old self isn't just what you were before your conversion; it's also what you were before you read this sentence. God is continually removing our past by His wonderful grace and making us "new."

But to have the blessings that come with that, you *have* to believe.

Not just believe that He exists, but believe that He can and will do what He says He will do.[22]

Neither positive thinking nor disciplined thinking can remove guilt, except on a temporary basis. But faith in what Jesus did for you can remove it forever and render the flesh powerless for the rest of your life. Please understand, I'm not playing on semantics here. Faith and positive thinking are not the same thing. Positive and disciplined thinking both rely on the power of the person.

131

Faith, on the other hand, does just the opposite. It recognizes the impotency of the person and the all-surpassing power of God. You can't take yourself into a healed spiritual state, but if you place your faith in Jesus, He will put you there.

If Jesus could forgive the sexually immoral, idolaters, adulterers, male prostitutes, homosexual offenders, thieves, the greedy, drunkards, slanderers, and swindlers,[23] He can, and will, forgive you.

Believe it.

When you do, you will be healed.

"YOU ARE CONTROLLED BY THE SPIRIT"

For more than twenty years, I've known and preached what I just wrote for you in the preceding section. Yet, in those same twenty years, I've experienced the worst sins of my life. How can that be? You see, the faith I'm describing isn't something you know only intellectually. It goes much deeper than that. It even goes deeper than the emotions, though both intellect and emotions are involved.

It goes all the way to the spirit.

Not just a person's spirit.

The Holy Spirit.

For years, I shied away from involvement with the Holy Spirit. I feared the condemnation of my fellowship of believers, who tend to discount the work of the Spirit. But after years of trying to fight the good fight by my own power, I was forced to look for help beyond myself. It was more necessity than theology that drove me. I needed the spiritual deliverance that I couldn't provide for myself—or for anyone who looked to me for help.

I tired of giving the same glib answers about how prayer, discipline, and accountability would solve all spiritual problems. Oh, I believe in prayer, discipline, and accountability, and they are essential tools; but they aren't a substitute for the power of God.

The Spirit Sets Us Free

Paul ended Romans 7 lamenting his inability to overcome sin because of the battle between his flesh and his mind, but he said in chapter 8, "The law of the Spirit of life set me free from the law of sin and death."[24] The answer has been there all along. For all of us. Freedom from sin and guilt is found in the "law of the Spirit of life."

The Power of God is Accessed by Faith

When you surrender in faith, that faith isn't just that God is there and that He forgives. It's also believing He'll take residence in you. God places His Spirit in each person He forgives and brings into His family.[25] That Spirit is the Holy Spirit. And His Spirit will control your mind, if you allow Him to.

When you surrender in faith, your mind will set itself on what the Spirit desires, not on what your flesh desires. Doubt that? Then read the following Scripture: "Those who live according to the sinful nature have their minds set on what that nature desires; but those who live in accordance with the Spirit have their minds set on what the Spirit desires. . . . The mind controlled by the Spirit is life and peace. . . . You . . . are controlled . . . by the Spirit, if the Spirit of God lives in you."[26]

It would take an entire book to explain how the Spirit of God controls the mind of those who are in Jesus. That's a book I look forward to writing; I wish I had the space right here to share all I've learned about it.

If you think being controlled by the Spirit is something you accomplish by having your mind set on what the Spirit desires, you misunderstand the passage quoted above. Paul's emphasis isn't that you somehow find the commands of God in Scripture and, by obeying them well enough, evidence the control of the Spirit in your life. He says that the *Spirit* will control your mind.

Do you have a voice in whether He does that?

Absolutely.

Notice that he points out that you can choose to live by the sinful nature. When you do that, your mind will devote itself to what that nature desires. Or you can choose to live by the Spirit. When you do that, your mind will devote itself to what He desires.

But the Spirit can go beyond the power of your mind. Beyond your decision to live by Him rather than by the flesh. When you yield to God in faith, His Spirit will dwell with you to the point of *controlling* your mind. When, by faith, you allow Him to do that, your flesh hasn't the power to compel you that it once held.

Believing that your sinful state is "rendered powerless" places you into a healed spiritual state. But it's not only the sense of forgiveness you have that makes the flesh less powerful, it's your surrender to the Spirit so that you are *controlled* by Him, so that you actually *live* according to the Spirit.[27]

While my mind and my spirit too often fall prey to the flesh, His Spirit in me carries more strength than a thousand sinful natures—a thousand times a thousand times a thousand.

And more beyond that.

When we, by faith, trust Jesus, trust that our old self is crucified, and trust that we are no longer who we were, we at last open ourselves to the leading of God.

When you become a Christian, God forgives you. Not because of what you've done, but because of what Jesus did for you on the cross. As He takes on Himself all you have done, your sin and all its consequences are gone forever. Quite literally, by His wounds you are healed.[28] And that moving of sin and guilt from you to

Him didn't occur once and for all at your conversion. It continues for the rest of your Christian life.

But if in your heart you refuse to believe that, you will suffer at least two spiritual diseases. You will continually sin, all your life, even as you despise yourself for it. And you will never experience the healing power of God that removes all guilt and shame.

Don't let that happen.

Surrender in faith to Jesus, and believe what He says about your forgiveness.

Start believing it now. If you are a Christian, tell yourself that God has wiped away all the wrong you've ever done. It's all gone forever. Even the sins you have committed since you first believed in Jesus, since your confession of Jesus as Lord. Even since you last prayed.

That's all there is to it.

Really.

By showing us how impossible it is to keep a law perfectly, God leads us directly to Jesus, who saves us despite our disobedience.

࿐

Therefore, since we have been justified through faith, we have peace with God through our Lord Jesus Christ, through whom we have gained access by faith into this grace in which we now stand. And we rejoice in the hope of the glory of God.

Romans 5:1–2

Believe That Mercy and Grace Are Yours

The woman had to know she wouldn't be welcome. More than that, she had to know she would set the whole town into a tizzy just by showing up. There were places where you could find women like her, but those places never included church.

Or the preacher's house.

At a party.

Especially when the party was in honor of a famous visiting evangelist, the most famous person who had ever been in that quiet little nowhere town.

Maybe there were other women at the party who did what she did. But they were refined; they knew the whens, wheres, whos, and hows of self-indulgent pleasure, and they wouldn't be caught. Their discreet activities were hidden in the darkness, shielded by the smokescreens of public piety and community involvement. Yes, I think they must have been there. After all, elite social circles have sinners too. Even in prestigious churches.

And at Pharisees' houses.

I've thought a lot about that party described in Luke 7, and I have made for myself a mental picture to help me understand what happened that day. May I share it with you?

I see those church women gathered at the party (I guess "synagogue women" might be more accurate, but thinking in terms of church helps me frame it into my world better). Some of them are genuinely good, kind, and holy. Some aren't. They stand just as guilty as the sinful lady who had the audacity to invite herself, but any secret involvement they share in her sins doesn't create compassion within them. Why should it? She doesn't fit into their circle. Her dress is too coarse, her language too common, her sin too known. She is an "across-the-tracks" sinner. None of them realizes any commonality with this vulgar woman walking through the gate toward the front steps of this godly home.

"She doesn't belong here," each thinks to herself. "What makes her think she can just waltz in here as brazenly as if this were a cheap hotel room with a waiting client? She isn't looking for religion, or she'd go to a church to find it. Surely some church around here caters to her kind. Maybe one on the seedy side of town. This is a private church party, and we don't want people like her here. The only reason she could be here is to flaunt herself. Simon won't put up with this. He'll tongue-lash her so badly she'll never try this stunt again."

Think I'm exaggerating in my little drama? I don't. That's how people reason when they exclude someone God tells them to love—indignation instead of inclusion. Castigation rather than concern.

Some of the men who see the woman coming think the same spiritually superior thoughts as their wives. Not quite as judgmentally, perhaps, but spiritually snobbish just the same. Other men blanch as they see her come through the door. Completely overwhelmed by panic, they stop midword and midgesture as though some evil spirit had instantly turned them to stone. They stand helpless, waiting to witness the scene that will end their marriages and make them the objects of cruel jokes for years to come.

She walks past them all.

She ignores their lifted noses and disapproving glares. She ignores the peculiarly sweet stench of panic. She moves past the servers, the onlookers, and the church hierarchy. As if unaware of anything or anyone around her, she walks on until she comes to the low table where the host and his special guest are already reclined across from each other, waiting for the meal to begin. Pausing only long enough to plan her path, she steps over dining guests and past other guests sitting or standing near the wall. She knows the custom; those standing weren't invited to eat, just to listen, and to see, and to be seen. Shamelessly nudging a place for herself between two people sitting directly behind the evangelist, she sinks to her knees before His feet.

She sees Him looking at her, smiling. She doesn't know why He's smiling and would never guess it is amusement at the way she'd plunged the room into silence by her determined entrance.

Jesus lies on his left side, positioned at an angle to the table, which stands about a foot high. He leans on his left elbow and lifts His cup with his right hand. It is a custom of the day, a rather relaxed way to enjoy a meal. The angle gives Him a perfect view of this woman kneeling just beyond the mat on which He reclines. She is close enough that if she bends at the waist, she can kiss His feet. After staring several seconds into His eyes, that's exactly what she does. Within a moment, servants place food and drink before Jesus, distracting his attention from the woman. Then, as if she weren't there, He starts to eat.

Eating doesn't come so easily for His host, who is staring in horror directly across the table.

Jesus eats anyway, making polite dinner conversation, pretending not to notice His host's obvious rage toward the woman at His feet—the woman who now cries softly as she continues to kiss those soiled feet.

Jesus could focus on any person in the room, read his thoughts, learn her heart. But there are two people who capture His attention: the sinful woman crying at His feet and the Pharisee who finds her so disquieting.

Without warning, Jesus feels hands brushing lightly across his ankles, slowly at first and then with more urgency. He doesn't start in surprise, nor does He look; He knows what the woman is doing. He's been expecting it. Her teardrops have made patterns in the dust that clings to His feet. Dust gathered from the walk to His host's house. Dust that proper etiquette dictated should have already been washed from Him. Dust now splattered with spilling sorrow. Instinctively, without conscious thought or consideration of His reaction to her violation of social mores by actually touching Him, she tries to remove the tracks of her tears. Her failure to make the marks go away makes her cry all the more. Sobbing now, wiping furiously, she is unable to control the flowing torrent. She doesn't think to lean back, wipe her eyes, and flee the room. Lost in her hurt, she keeps dropping her pain onto Jesus' feet and trying to remove it with the caress of her hand.

Jesus eats. Still ignoring her, He looks sadly at Simon.

Simon doesn't look sad at all. That's because he doesn't feel the woman's sadness. He's too angry at the spectacle before him—a harlot in his house and a so-called prophet who doesn't have the sense to know what she is! She's kissing His feet, and He doesn't recoil in revulsion! And now—O God in heaven how can this be?—now she's taking down her hair. In public! Does she know no shame? She's wiping His feet with her hair!

For her, it's the next logical step in her illogical behavior. She's cried herself dry. There are no tears left to fall. Her crying has completely cleaned the dust from Jesus' feet. Now, looking for some cloth to dry Him, she finds nothing clean enough on her dress or within the recesses of her garments. Still kissing those blessed feet, she lifts her right hand to the covering on her head—not to use it for drying but to remove it. She makes no pause in her kissing as she slides her headcovering down her back. As soon as it is out of the way, she loosens the bands that hold her hair and shakes her head while lifting her face to allow her hair to tumble free. No Jewish woman would ever do that in public, and here she has done it in the Pharisee's house! Perhaps some men in that room had seen her unfettered hair before—men who, if they weren't so afraid, would find themselves stirred by the memory the sight brings. She seems not to care. If she, on occasion, has allowed her companion sinners to see her as she is, why should she hide anything from her Savior? Besides, her hair is the cleanest thing available to her, and she is not going to touch Him with anything dirty.

She dries His feet while continuing to kiss Him—kissing His ankle, kissing His toes, kissing any part of Him she can reach. Not in passion. Not for money. Not like any kisses she has given any man in any secret time of her sordid life. They are kisses of total brokenness.

Once her task is completed, she takes perfume and massages it into His olive-colored skin. It never crosses her mind that her actions are similar to those she's done before in shame. She feels shame now, but it isn't because of what she is doing, only for what she has done. She offers herself to this man in a completely different manner from which she has offered herself to men before. She isn't offering her body. She offers instead her heart, her mind, her soul.

But Jesus doesn't speak to her, doesn't acknowledge her presence. He is seemingly oblivious to her actions. Instead, He speaks to the self-righteous Pharisee who at that very moment is thinking, "If this man were a prophet, he would know who is touching him and what kind of woman she is—that she is a sinner."[1]

Jesus, reading his thoughts, shakes His head in divine dismay and tells him a story about cancelled debts and love, a story that will hit Simon and every guest in that house hard. At its conclusion, Jesus turns his head toward the woman, but He speaks to Simon. "Do you see this woman?"[2]

Even in this tension-filled room, Jesus displays His gentle humor by asking the question. He acts as if Simon hasn't noticed this uninvited guest or her shocking behavior. No, He isn't being insensitive to the woman at His feet. He let her hurt as long as she needed to, but now He's going to give her joy. It's okay to use humor. A time of rejoicing is near.

Still speaking to Simon, Jesus continues,

> I came into your house. You did not give me any water for my feet, but she wet my feet with her tears and wiped them with her hair. You did not give me a kiss, but this woman, from the time I entered, has not stopped kissing my feet. You did not put oil on my head, but she has poured perfume on my feet. Therefore, I tell you, her many sins have been forgiven—for she loved much. But he who has been forgiven little loves little.[3]

The woman stops kissing His feet, raises her head, and stares at Him in open-mouthed disbelief. Thoughts flood her. "Did He say forgiven? Did He say I have been forgiven? Me?"

Jesus unlocks His eyes from Simon's then locks them intently on hers, making sure she grasps the message: "Your sins are forgiven."[4]

He knows she needs to hear it directly from Him. He knows that she finds it beyond imagination that God can forgive someone like her, someone who's spent so many years in such flagrant sin, someone who has no excuse for her sins, only a longing for her future and a fleeing from her past.

So He tells her again, "Your faith has saved you; go in peace."[5] Her faith. That's what led Him to remove her legal guilt. Her faith, if she believes Him, will also remove her personal guilt. With both relieved, she can go in peace. The kind of peace only He could offer.

I can only assume she did. If Jesus told me I was forgiven, I would walk away with peace in my heart. You would too.

Or, at least you would if you believed Him.

The trouble is that many of us just can't believe that Jesus' words of forgiveness are for us. We think there must be some huge deed we must do or some punishment we must suffer. Something we must do to earn forgiveness. We just can't believe it's as simple as "Your faith has saved you; go in peace." Our human nature says there has to be more.

In actuality, it's not simple at all. Our salvation came at a great price; it's just that *we* don't have to pay the price. It's already been paid.

In order to understand how this could be so, we need to take a closer look at the concept of faith and works.

GRACE/FAITH VS. LAW/WORKS

To grasp the New Testament teaching about forgiveness, we must understand the difference between its system of salvation and that of the Old Testament. The New Testament system may be called *grace/faith*. The Old Testament system could generally be referred to as *law/works*. There are basic and essential differences between the two. The most important one is that we can find salvation under grace/faith but only condemnation under law/works.

Under a system of law/works, we must perfectly obey the law by our works (or obedience to the law) in order to earn the blessing of God. *Any* violation of the law brings condemnation. Obedience to the law earns us a degree of righteousness. If we keep the law perfectly, we are saved by the law through the efficacy of our own deeds.

On the other hand, a system of grace/faith anticipates that we will not perfectly obey the law. Under this system there is also a law; that part doesn't change. The difference is that salvation is not earned by obedience. While perfect obedience is commanded, provision is made for imperfect obedience. Sin, while soundly condemned, is anticipated and removed by God as He sees living faith in sinners. Therefore, we are saved neither by the law nor by obedience to the law (works). We are saved by the grace of God because of faith.

Law/Works

The Law of Moses in the Old Testament was established on a law/works platform. If a person obeyed the Law of Moses perfectly, God would bless and save that person. Any unrighteous works—disobedience to *any* law of God—would condemn the person to lose God's blessing and salvation. In short, salvation was established by perfect obedience. Legal and personal guilt were removed by a person's own actions. It would be a great law to live under if you could live perfectly.

Glad you're not under that law? Me too! God gave that law to prove to humankind that salvation through a law/works system would *not* work! No one—not you, not your teacher, not even your mother—will live in perfect obedience. The people who lived under the Law of Moses didn't, and we won't today. The only one who ever did is Jesus, and that's one of the things about Him that shows Him capable of becoming the atoning sacrifice for the rest of us.

In Galatians 3, the apostle Paul explained why no one of us will perfectly obey the law. Through this letter to the churches in the

Galatia area, God teaches plainly that a law/works theology brings doom and damnation on all who try to live by it. By the Spirit, Paul wrote, "All who rely on observing the law are under a curse, for it is written: 'Cursed is everyone who does not continue to do everything written in the Book of the Law.' Clearly, no one is justified before God by the law."[6]

Even as Paul wrote these words, he knew that people sold on a law/works mind-set would not agree. They were well aware that they didn't keep the law with perfect obedience, but they had figured a way around it. They simply obeyed what they considered to be "essential" laws so that they could violate without remorse laws they considered "optional." They actually seemed to believe they could earn salvation with righteous acts, if they were the *right* righteous acts. While giving lip service to the idea that no one can keep the law perfectly, they behaved as if it could be done. No, not by never sinning, but by negating sin through specific acts of righteousness. They considered themselves not guilty of legal sin when they broke the law because they meticulously obeyed certain other commands, which they insisted meant they hadn't "really" broken the law at all. Of course, since they believed they carried no legal guilt, they felt no personal guilt.

Think I'm making this up?

Read the condemnations Jesus gave to the Pharisees' manipulations of God's law that made them believe they were saved by their obedience. Here's how Jesus addressed one such situation:

> You say that if a man says to his father or mother, "Whatever help you might otherwise have received from me is a gift devoted to God," he is not to "honor his father" with it. Thus you nullify the word of God for the sake of your tradition. You hypocrites! Isaiah was right when he prophesied about you: "These people honor me with their lips,

but their hearts are far from me. They worship me in vain; the teachings are but rules taught by men."[7]

They dismissed their failure to honor their parents by making a gift to God. They "kept" the law while violating it. They viewed honoring God as a matter of essential doctrine and relegated the command to honor their parents to a list of commands not essential to their salvation.

They called that obedience.

Jesus called it hypocrisy.

Don't be shocked by the goings-on of the people in Jesus' day. People still do it today. I run across it regularly, don't you? Some folks who claim Christianity believe very much in a law/works salvation. You would think their belief would make them very careful to do just what God commands, but they too pick and choose the commands they deem crucial. Just like the Pharisees.

When I was a young preacher, I sat helplessly in a meeting where Christians soundly condemned other Christians in a church down the street because they did some things differently from the way we did them. The angry men in that room wrapped unconnected verses together into a tapestry of alleged evidence, discussed intricate and obscure meanings of Greek words they had never met, and drew conclusions as to the fate of those churches who reached a different conclusion than they.

The gathered group very much lived by a law/works system, but I didn't notice because I'd been trained to do the same. They proclaimed that we are not to take from or add to the Word and that a person guilty of one sin is guilty of all. They made it clear that God in heaven cannot stomach people who claim to follow Him but don't get all His commands just right, because *every* command is to be obeyed exactly or salvation will be lost. After all, none of us would even be here if Noah had mistakenly included a pine plank—rather than the commanded cypress wood—in the ark! One slip and it's over—no matter how good your intentions.

Being younger and more naive, I bought into all that, but I became confused by the implications. "Brothers, I see your point. A Christian should obey every law of God, whatever that law might be. So, why aren't we just as strongly condemning the sin of those in our church who don't tell others about Jesus. He commanded that very specifically. And what about some in our congregation who gossip and spread tales. I've got some good verses on that. And . . ."

With gentle words they stopped me. Obviously I had a lot to learn. Yes, God commanded those things as well, but they weren't nearly as important as those crucial commands disobeyed by the folks down the street. Some things are just more important than others—some things are "matters of faith," while others are just "matters of opinion." On and on they went until I dropped my contention. I knew something was wrong with that kind of reasoning, but I just couldn't figure out what it was. Nor would I be able to until I abandoned trying to get to heaven by a law/works system.

It appears that *anyone* living under law/works has to build a tier of important and unimportant commands. Why? Because no one can keep the whole law of God perfectly. Since that is impossible, each person or group who thinks their obedience will save them *must* pick a handful of commands they think essential and concentrate on them to the exclusion of the rest. Otherwise, even they cannot delude themselves into thinking that obedience to the commands of God earns them the blessing they crave.

But what happens when they violate the laws they deem crucial? After all, since they are human they must fail in those areas, too, on occasion.

Those who believe in law/works salvation obviously find themselves in major spiritual trouble when they commit any sin they knew better than to do and recognize it as a sin. But never fear, as soon as they ask God to forgive them, they regain their salvation! (Though some of them believe that public sin must be publicly confessed before God forgives.) They still seek salvation through law/works. See? They don't see confession as the natural response of a sorrowful Christian. They see it as a required act of obedience that immediately *obligates* God to forgive them. Still saved by obedience. They got themselves into legal guilt by their sin, but they remove their guilt by praying or confessing publicly. (Interestingly, they don't necessarily believe that the confession brings them back into acceptance by the righteous. It just saves them; it doesn't mean the righteous have to treat them as equals.) By viewing confession this way, they keep intact their belief that a person is always saved by obedience! They actually believe that they can be forgiven of their sins by their own actions. "I know I sinned, but that's okay because I confessed my sin and now God must forgive me." For them, salvation is always a legal contract. I must do my part. God must do his. I get to heaven by fulfilling the stipulations of the contract.

But that view is totally wrong. Nothing we can do earns our salvation—not even confession. God looks only for our faith—our living faith.

"Wait a minute!" you may object. "It *is* my obedience that saves me. After all, doesn't Philippians tell us to 'work out' our own salvation?"

Evidently you didn't notice that when Paul told us to "work out" our salvation, he continued the sentence with, "for it is God who works in you to will and to act according to his good purpose."[8] Paul didn't contradict what he said in so many other places, such as Ephesians 2:8–9. You can never "work out" your salvation by anything *you* do; *God* works in you. Yes, you should obey. But never think that in this passage Paul ever implied that the quality or quantity of your obedience earns your salvation. He said it flatly in the Ephesian passage, "not from yourselves . . . not by works."

So why did God give a law that we can't keep? A law that brings us condemnation?

The Law Brings Us to Christ

The law God gave in the Old Testament through Moses served a dual purpose. The first purpose was to govern their society. When the children of Israel left Egypt, they no longer had the Egyptian laws to govern their society. Just like any nation gaining independence, they needed laws to prevent chaos.

Paul said the law was added because of "transgression."[9] People had to know what was right and what was wrong. And they had to know the penalty for wrong. So God gave them a law that encompassed the spiritual, medical, social, and legal aspects of life.

But the Law of Moses was much more than that. It had a second purpose. Beyond telling the people how to live, it included ordinances that proved to them that they could never obey it well enough to enter heaven. God designed the Law of Moses to show His people they were sinners in need of salvation. Imperfect and lost by themselves, they needed something more.

Of course, that "something more" is Jesus.

Here's how Paul explained it: "What, then, was the purpose of the law? It was added because of transgressions until the Seed to whom the promise referred had come."[10] God never intended the law given through Moses to bring His people to salvation. He would send Jesus, the Seed, to do that. Bringing people to heaven was never its purpose. That's why Paul said, "The law was put in charge to lead us to Christ that we might be justified by faith,"[11] and, "Through him everyone who believes is justified from everything you could not be justified from by the law of Moses."[12]

"For if a law had been given that could impart life, then righteousness would certainly have come by the law. But the Scripture declares that the whole world is a prisoner of sin, so that what was promised, being given through faith in Jesus Christ, might be given to those who believe."[13] Here is the key: *Righteousness only comes through faith in Jesus Christ, not from obeying the law!*

By showing us how impossible it is to keep a law perfectly, God leads us directly to Jesus, who saves us despite our disobedience. Yes, that's right, despite our disobedience. You'll never obey the law well enough to get to heaven. Only Jesus can get you there.

If you have faith in Him.

What about the "Perfect Law of Liberty"?

Some will agree that we cannot be saved by the Law of Moses but believe we are saved by the "perfect law of liberty," mentioned in James 1:25. They see a difference between the Old Testament law and the New Testament law.

If you believe this, you are still in a law/works mode rather than a grace/faith mode. While the passages I've quoted from Galatians 3 refer specifically to the Law of Moses, the principle is carried forth throughout the New Testament: *It's impossible for obedience to any law to save you.* You are not saved by your actions but by God's grace given because of your faith. Paul tells us what we earn from our actions: He says we earn death.[14]

We cannot be saved by obeying a law.

Not the Old Testament Law of Moses.

Not the New Testament "law of liberty."

Abraham's Justification Proves Works Don't Save

The Spirit so much wants us to understand this principle that He elaborated on it clearly through the apostle Paul in Romans 4. Discussing Abraham, father of the faithful, Paul pointed out that he received neither his position in history nor his favor with God by his obedience. He said,

> If, in fact, Abraham was justified by works, he had something to boast about—but not before God. What does the Scripture say? "Abraham believed God, and it was credited to him as righteousness." Now when a man works, his wages are not credited to him as a gift, but as an obligation. However, to the man who does not work but trusts God who justifies the wicked, his faith is credited as righteousness.[15]

Paul stated unequivocally that Abraham was not justified by his obedience (works) but by his faith. God owed Abraham nothing, just as He owes us nothing. Well, let me restate that. He does owe us something: The wages we have earned for ourselves is death! But He surely doesn't owe us life or heaven or any such thing.

Paul used Abraham, the father of the Jewish nation, to prove His point because converted Jews coming from a law/works mind-set were trying to combine their reliance on the law with their newfound faith in Christ. Paul was well acquainted with the Jewish law/works system. He grew up with it. So he hit the Jews with a grace/faith bombshell.

As these Jewish converts knew, Abraham had been commanded to circumcise all the males in his entourage, including himself. Under a system of law/works, Abraham could only be justified when he obeyed the command. Obey the stipulations of the contract; get the reward. But Paul said Abraham was counted righteous *before* he obeyed the circumcision command.[16] Paul called Abraham's circumcision a "seal of the righteousness that he had by faith while he was still uncircumcised."[17]

We know from having read Genesis 17:14 that circumcision was essential. God would "cut off from his people" any male who wasn't circumcised as one who "has broken my covenant." Abraham could never relegate it to some secondary status. Yet even obeying that essential command was not what made Abraham right with God. It was his faith.

Not law.

Faith.

When Paul used Abraham as proof that justification didn't come by law, he was not referring to the Law of Moses, since that law wouldn't exist for hundreds of years after Abraham. Paul used the word *law* to mean the commands of God. And Paul said, "It was not through law that Abraham and his offspring received the promise that he would be heir of the world, but through the righteousness that comes by faith."[18]

If God saved us because of our obedience to His commands rather than the faith He sees in our hearts, He could not have justified Abraham until after Abraham was circumcised! By justifying him before the act, God demonstrated that the faith in our hearts that precedes the act of obedience is more important to Him than the act of obedience itself. And that, of course, means that He doesn't intend for us to live by law/works.

GRACE/FAITH

Under a system of law/works, a person must be perfectly obedient to be saved. Under a system of grace/faith, perfect obedience is not anticipated, although it is commanded. God gives grace to those who believe in Him. "It is by grace you have been saved, through faith—and this not from yourselves, it is the gift of God—not by works, so that no one can boast."[19]

Can the Spirit of God, through Paul, make it any plainer than that? God wants us to obey—expects us to obey—but our salvation isn't dependent on the quantity or quality of our obedience. Salvation and forgiveness come to those who trust Jesus.

The two words most used in the discussion of forgiveness are *grace* and *mercy*. What exactly do these words mean? Are they two ways to describe the same thing, or do they mean different things altogether?

Let's define them simply.

Mercy is when God *doesn't* give you what you *do* deserve.

Grace is when God *does* give you what you *don't* deserve.

Here's an illustration that may help. Several years ago, while passing the town of Opelika, Alabama, on Interstate 20, I carelessly allowed myself to drive faster than the speed limit. It was so long ago my car radio only received the AM band, and I'd been fiddling with the tuner trying to find music to keep me awake. Strange as it may seem, around 5:00 A.M. I happened upon a station from Columbus, Georgia, whose announcer was totally unchained to convention. Although it was August, he played a Christmas song. Really. "Rudolf the Red-Nosed Reindeer." Happy for the diversion, I sang merrily along and, in the process, unwittingly allowed myself to creep higher and higher above the speed limit.

What was a state trooper doing out there that time of the morning anyway?

Braking to a stop on the side of the road, I grabbed my wallet, pulled myself out of the car, and hurried to the patrol car behind me. After all, I didn't want him outside in that cold Christmas weather. The trooper motioned me into the passenger seat, took my license, asked me if I knew how fast I was going, and began to write the ticket. During our brief conversation, I noticed his nametag and realized I knew him. (I'm changing the name here so he won't be tempted to shoot me.) Just as he started to write, I spoke—timidly at first, but ending boldly.

"You're Charlie Smith, aren't you? I mean the Charlie Smith I met at a church here in Opelika a few months back when I attended a revival? I'm a preacher from over in LaGrange, Georgia, and I've been to your church several times.

"Boy, Charlie, it's good to meet a brother on the road!"

Charlie stared at me for several seconds, sighed, and slipped his ticket book onto the seat beside him. Picking up another book, he asked, "If I give you a warning ticket, will you promise me you won't speed anymore until you get out of the state of Alabama?"

It was only thirty miles; I figured I could do it.

Charlie wrote me a warning ticket and let me go.

Now, here's the question: Did Charlie show me grace, mercy, or both?

He showed me mercy. He didn't give me what I deserved. I deserved a sixty-four dollar speeding ticket. How do I know? Because just a few weeks later, my wife was stopped at the same place, and the trooper gave her a sixty-four dollar speeding ticket.

She got what she deserved!

It would have been grace added to mercy if Charlie had not only let me go but had also said, "Mr. Beam, congratulations. You're the hundred-thousandth speeder stopped in Alabama this month, and as part of our tourism program, the great State of Alabama wants to give you one hundred thousand dollars. Not only that; you get your own state-trooper car. Flip on the lights and siren and drive as fast as you want, anywhere you want. And, to top it all off, you get your own state trooper Smokey Bear hat!"

If a state trooper told you that after stopping you for speeding, you might think he'd been in one too many car chases.

But that's what mercy and grace do. Mercy doesn't punish you for what you've done wrong. Grace gives you glorious presents instead of the punishment you should have received. People typically don't work like that; God always does. At least He always does to His children who are living by faith.

Such actions go so far beyond human comprehension that we find them difficult to accept. Hence, our current study. We doubt that God will bring us into a healed spiritual state because we don't grasp how He can give us mercy, much less grace. We wait breathlessly for His punishment, and He gently hands us a blessing.

Is this as hard for you to accept as it is for me? Not only will God *not* punish me for the sin, He will continue blessing me even as I struggle with sin! If any human has treated me like that consistently, I don't recall it. Oh, some have tried. Some have even done it for a while. But we humans have a hard time forgiving, much less going out of our way to provide a blessing for the person sinning against us.

God does that when He gives grace. Grace isn't just the joy of heaven gained when death quietly sips the last breath from our lungs. God's grace gives us good things while we're still here. We have a graceful God who answers the prayers of struggling Christians who fear that God doesn't want to hear from them. He puts good people, good times, and good news into the lives of His children who deserve nothing. And who expect something terrible.

Mercy would be wonderful enough, but He wants to give us more. A gift. Many gifts. None deserved. He sees our sin and opens the windows of heaven to us in spite of our failings.

Too good to be true?

A grasp of the glory of grace comes only by faith. You believe it because God said it. If you try to figure it out, it all falls apart. We think like humans, and humans don't think like God. Therefore, we have to believe what He said is true whether it makes sense to us or not.

Grace and mercy don't exist under a system of law/works. But they are absolutely essential under a system of grace/faith. How else could all us sinners find God's favor and forgiveness? We can only have it if He gives it to us as a gift. Grace. A gift. The gift of God.

Why am I making such a big deal about this?

Because so many believers claim to be saved by grace, but they really believe in their hearts that they are saved by their obedience. Not only is this extremely frustrating to those who try to live by such spiritual nonsense, it borders on being accursed by God. Remember what Paul said in Galatians: "All who rely on observing the law are under a curse."[20] In fury, the Spirit wrote through Paul that people who taught that heinous heresy were to be "eternally condemned."[21]

You can't have it both ways. Either you're justified by obeying law, or you're justified by faith in Christ. If you choose justification by your own obedience, then you are placing your faith in yourself. Is that what you really want? Would you really choose faith in your obedience over faith in Christ?

Yes, God commands us to obey Him, but when we fall short, He forgives and offers us heaven anyway.

Quit feeling guilty about failing to keep the law. Mourn your sin, then accept God's forgiveness. Quit worrying that you haven't done enough to earn heaven. Accept the fact that God isn't looking for perfect obedience; He's looking for *living faith.* Be His workmanship. Work because He saved you. Obey so you will know your faith is alive. When you work like that, you'll finally be working for Him.

And when you fail, as you will because of your humanity, remember that "if anybody does sin, we have one who speaks to the Father in our defense—Jesus Christ, the Righteous One. He is the atoning sacrifice for our sins."[22]

God doesn't demand perfect
obedience because He knows
we can't give it. He sees our
direction, forged by living
faith, and grants us mercy.

*I write these things to you who believe in
the name of the Son of God so that you
may know that you have eternal life.*

1 John 5:13

CHAPTER 8

Believe God's Assurances

Although I had arrived several hours earlier, the man in the next bed had hardly spoken. He glanced at me as I entered the room, watching only for a moment before turning back toward the window, and hadn't looked my direction since. Not that I had time to visit anyway. No sooner did I enter than the nurse pulled the curtain so I could disrobe in private and slip into the new pajamas Alice had bought for my stay. (For some unimaginable reason she didn't think my regular bed ensemble suitable for a hospital visit.) I grudgingly slipped into them, griping under my breath the whole time, then just as grudgingly offered my body to the indignities of modern medical science. Various professionals poked, prodded, measured, and jotted until they bored themselves with the project and reluctantly ambled down the hall to find some other soul to torment.

The stranger next to the window paid me no attention at all. He didn't read. Didn't watch television. Didn't do anything. Just lay there staring out the window at nothing. His wife sat next to his bed, holding his hand, occasionally speaking to him in tones too subdued to hear.

I assumed that he faced surgery the following day, just as I did. The nurses had informed me this was the surgical wing and that I would be returning to my same bed after the operation. Every patient on this wing did, unless he was moved directly into intensive care.

Several visitors came to see me in the early evening hours. Some to pray. Some to joke. All to let me know they were thinking of me. Each acknowledged my roommate and his wife with a nod or a smile or a cordial greeting, but they made no response.

It was after the nurses swept the stragglers away, including both my Alice and my taciturn roommate's wife, that we were finally alone. I didn't want to be alone, so I tried to make contact. "Surgery tomorrow?"

To my mild surprise he answered, "Yeah."

"Me too," I muttered.

I hoped for a longer response, or maybe a bit of conversation now that the door was open, but he said nothing more. He continued to look out the window into darkness. As I watched him, my gregariousness evolved into a desire to minister, but I felt I had no right to intrude. It wasn't a night for the mindlessness of TV, so we each lay in the semidarkness hospitals allow and faced our fears.

Alone.

"You a preacher?" he asked after several minutes.

"Yeah." I responded. In those days I was.

"I thought you were. I heard ya'll talkin'. Can I ask you a question . . . I mean . . . wouldya' mind?"

"Fire away," I replied. "I can't promise you I'll know the answer, but I'll give it my best shot. What would you like to know?"

"Tomorrow . . . tomorrow morning they're goin' after a brain tumor they think is cancer. They already told me that I go to

160

intensive care if I . . . ah . . . if I survive the surgery. They told me and my wife that I might not make it through 'cause of where they gotta cut.

"I think I might die in the mornin'."

"Oh." I was too embarrassed to say more, conscious of how my retinue of boisterous visitors must have frustrated him as he tried to spend what might have been his last night on earth quietly holding his wife's hand.

"Preacher. I need some help with sumpin'. I'm a Christian. Gave my heart to Jesus when I was fifteen and never looked back. But I ain't been perfeck. Sometimes my wife deserved a lot better than she got. Kids, too. I swear when I get real mad, and I've been known to take a drink or two. But I love Jesus, and I want to go to heaven. I go to church. I've helped people all my life. I read my Bible and even taught a Sunday school class or two over the years. I ain't been a bad man, but I ain't been no Mother Teresa either.

"Tell me, preacher," his voice faltered slightly, a strong man trying not to show fear, "you think I'll go to heaven if I die tomorrow?"

We talked well into the night, pausing only when the nurses came in to take a temperature or squeeze out a blood-pressure reading. When they would leave, we'd talk on. I asked him about his conversion, about his life, about his faith, and about his love. He was too apprehensive to slant his story toward sainthood. He told it like it was because he figured he might meet an angel of death within hours. He wanted to know what would happen if he did.

Maybe I didn't need to ask so much. Hear so much. But it's one thing to tell a person in a counseling session he's saved. It's quite another to tell a man about to find out the accuracy of your prediction.

Finally, I assured him, "Mister, I think I know a lot about you now. At least enough that you won't think what I'm about to say is 'preacher talk.' If the Bible is true, you'll go to heaven if you die tomorrow.

"And I believe the Bible is true.

"I'll pray for you now and pray for you in the morning until they put me to sleep. I'll pray that God will keep you alive for your wife and kids. Give you some more good years of doing good for people. But if you die, give God my regards, 'cause that's where you're going. Don't doubt your salvation, brother. You're God's child."

He didn't say any more. Just a muffled "thank you" choked through tightened vocal cords. I never saw him again, and because of my own circumstances, never found out if he lived or died.

I hoped he lived.

If he didn't, I'm sure God took him to heaven.

May I offer you some of the same counsel I offered the man in the hospital? Will you allow God to assure you of your salvation?

You can find God's assurance of your salvation several places in the New Testament. But in this chapter, we will look specifically at the assurances found in 1 John. We go there because one of John's expressed purposes for writing that epistle is to assure Christians that they have eternal life: "I write these things to you who believe in the name of the Son of God so that you may know that you have eternal life."[1]

Doubting salvation is doubting God, since salvation is His work and not ours. If He saved us based on what we accomplish, it would make sense for us to doubt, because we are not always to be trusted. But salvation is based on what God accomplished—from the promise made in the Garden to Eve and Adam to the Savior hanging on a cross—and God is always to be trusted.

To remove any doubt, John gives several assurances to us in this short letter. Assurances that every Christian should hear again and again.

ASSURANCE # 1: YOU ARE CONTINUALLY PURIFIED FROM SIN

"If we walk in the light, as he is in the light, we have fellowship with one another, and the blood of Jesus, his Son, purifies us from all sin."[2] The word translated as "purifies" in the New International Version is translated as "cleanseth" in the King James Version and "cleanses" in the New American Standard Version. John tells us that all of us who are "in the light" with Jesus reap two benefits or blessings from being in that light. The first is that we have "fellowship with one another," and the second is that Jesus, through His death, "purifies us from all sin." We are washed clean of our transgressions.

Notice that he didn't say "puri*fied*," meaning something that happened once and doesn't happen again. He puri*fies*. It keeps on happening throughout our walk with Jesus.

How can God do that? How can He keep me spiritually clean even when I fail to obey Him? Well, I don't intend to explain God since I don't have either the knowledge or privilege. But if we believe what He revealed, we get some insight into how God can continually cleanse us. It starts by removing our past so that we have a new future.

When Jesus allowed Himself to be nailed to that cross, "God made him who had no sin to be sin for us, so that in him we might become the righteousness of God."[3] That means that whatever I have done is what Jesus became on the cross. Same for you. He became what I was so that I can be what He is.

Holy.

Adulterers are no longer adulterers when they come to Jesus. He became an adulterer on the cross in their stead. He became a liar, thief, murderer, and child abuser. He became everything that He would ever forgive. He had no sin of His own, but the Father "made Him . . . to be sin for us." That means that as a Christian I don't have to die for my sin[4] on Judgment Day because Jesus already died for that sin. "One died for all, and therefore all died."[5] The penalty is paid; I don't owe it anymore. It is gone.

Removed.

Abolished.

Annihilated.

Therefore, Jesus died for every sin we committed before our conversions. But He did more than that. He also died for all the sins we commit *after* conversion. He not only forgives what we were. He keeps forgiving what we do. He promised it to all of us living in His light.

ASSURANCE #2: IF YOU DO SIN, YOU HAVE AN ADVOCATE

God doesn't want us to think that continual cleansing offers some kind of license to live godlessly. After telling us of the remarkable, continual forgiveness, John pauses to say, "My dear children, I write this to you so that you will not sin."[6] He doesn't want any of us to sin because that is contrary to the will of God. Paul gave the same message in Romans 6. God saved you, not so that you can sin more, but so that you might overcome the sinful nature by considering your past finished and over.

If John had stopped with the admonition for us not to sin, we would find ourselves in the midst of misery. True, we try not to sin. But sin sometimes comes in spite of ourselves—even when we consider our "old self" crucified with Christ. We try, but we fail.

If John—or more accurately, the Spirit writing through John—expected us to live in sinless perfection, too much was asked. No human can do it.[7]

Maybe the following illustration can make this clearer. It isn't nearly as intense as some I've shared, but it demonstrates that everyone—no matter what age—lacks the ability to be good. Just days before I wrote this chapter, my youngest daughter, Kimberly, age eight, was tormenting my second youngest daughter, Joanna, age twenty. Joanna was home for the weekend, taking a break from her studies at Faulkner University. Now, Kimberly is growing up in an adult world, and she thinks of herself as far older than a mere second-grader. Brilliant beyond her peers and somewhat spoiled by her doting parents, she can be quite demanding. She's smart enough and persistent enough to get her way most of the time. As she badgered Joanna to yield to her demands, I reasoned with her, "Kimberly, Joanna only gets to come home from school for short periods. Try not to aggravate her while she's here."

She explained with all the genuineness of an eight-year-old, "I *am* trying not to aggravate her!"

And she meant it.

The struggle in her mind between wanting the undivided attention of the sister she adores and wanting to allow that same sister some peace was more than she could control. Conflicting emotions created conflicting actions.

Our struggles typically reach greater dimensions than Kimberly's, but they follow the same pattern: conflict between two wanted things leads to conflict in our actions. We laugh at it in a child. We cry over it in ourselves.

So John follows the command that we not sin with assurance for us when we fail to obey perfectly. "But if anybody does sin, we have one who speaks to the Father in our defense—Jesus Christ, the Righteous One."[8] That phrase "one who speaks to the Father in our defense" comes from the Koine Greek word *parakletos*. It generally means "one who appears in another's behalf, mediator, intercessor, helper," and in some writings of the first century, it is interpreted as "attorney" or "lawyer."[9]

God commands us not to sin but knows that until we shed our flesh we will always have the inclination to commit sin. Therefore, He appointed, as it were, a defense attorney to represent us. Our advocate who speaks in our defense is none other than Jesus, the Righteous Son of God.

Talk about a legal "dream team"!

When our advocate speaks on our behalves, He will not seek acquittal on the grounds that we didn't do the crimes. He'll argue for total justification—a "not guilty" verdict—because the penalty for our crimes has already been paid. For evidence, our defense attorney will lift nail-scarred hands and point to a spear-pierced side.

"Yes," He'll say, "they did it. But they should be declared not guilty and allowed into all the wonders of heaven because they've already died in payment for the sin. Each of them died when I died. It happened as each in turn by faith accessed My death on the cross.[10] Don't punish them further. Tell them, 'Well done, good and faithful servants!'"[11]

And God will welcome us into His heaven.

Why will God let sinners like us in? Because, by His grace, He never looked for perfection from any of us; just direction. He isn't looking for perfect obedience because none of us can give it. He sees our direction (our seeking Him), forged by living faith, and grants mercy. He sees it and grants grace.

Grace for those sins we committed before we became Christians. Grace for those sins we've committed since. Grace for us when we violate His command that we not sin.

ASSURANCE #3: YOU KNOW IT'S SAVING FAITH IF IT'S *ALIVE*

In his plan to reassure us, John writes, "We have come to know him if we obey his commands."[12]

"Reassurance?" someone cries. "There's no reassurance in that. You just shared the verses that told us we *can't* perfectly obey! How can we know Him, if we have to perfectly obey Him to have that relationship?"

If you feel that way, just settle down. No reason to panic. John isn't contradicting all the other passages that say we have relationship with God because of our faith. He doesn't contemplate here that our salvation or our Christian walk is conditional upon complying perfectly with all the commands of God. He phrases this truth as he does because he wrote to an area plagued by Gnostics who said that they *didn't* have to obey God; as a matter of fact, they insisted they *didn't* even sin! They claimed their flesh was beyond their control, so anything the flesh did wasn't their responsibility. Therefore, they neither confessed sin nor obeyed God. John was right to tell them the same thing we should hear, "Obey God!" But he didn't expect them or us to interpret his message in a way that says God saves us because of the quantity or quality of our obedience. God saves us through faith. Paul taught it and John agrees, "This is the victory that has overcome the world, even our faith."[13]

How is it that we are saved by faith if God also commands us to obey Him? Why doesn't He save us based on the obedience we render rather than basing it on the faith in our hearts?

As we begin to study the answer, please remember this: If God saves us based on our obedience, we earn the salvation. If He saves us based on the living faith He sees in our hearts, He gives us salvation as a gift.

A gift—that's what grace is.

Sometimes Christians get confused because they misunderstand certain passages—specifically a few found in James. "In the same way, faith by itself, if it is not accompanied by action, is dead . . . You see that a person is justified by what he does and not by faith alone.[15] . . . As the body without the spirit is dead, so faith without deeds is dead."[16]

Some folks misapply these passages to teach that while we are saved by grace through faith, it isn't *only* faith that God examines. He looks "through" the faith to see the works that faith produces. Those "works of obedience" bring about our justification. Why then grace? They answer that your obedience gets you a percentage of the way toward heaven and God's grace makes up the rest. For example, your obedience may get you 72 percent of the way there and grace provides the missing 28 percent.

Of course, those verses don't teach any such heresy, and that is easy to see when they are studied in their context. First in the context of the book of James. Second in the context of the rest of the New Testament.

Does it make sense to interpret the lengthily explained teaching of Paul about salvation by grace through faith[17] by the guidance of the brief statement in James? Of course not. Paul explained himself—or should I say the Spirit explained Himself—very well. We are not saved by our works. Paul dealt with matters more theological (especially in Romans) while James dealt with matters more practical, such as actually living the commands of God rather than just knowing them.[18]

So, then, what did James tell us about faith and works? What do those verses mean in context of the letter James wrote?

James simply taught Christians to follow God with a living faith, for a dead faith isn't faith at all. He told us how we can know whether our faith is alive or dead. He, like Paul, saw faith as the key to justification by grace. Notice the phrasing. When he spoke of a dead faith he said, "Can such faith save him?"[19] That question falls immediately behind his words, "What good is it, my brothers, if a man claims to have faith but has no deeds?" Did you see that he didn't say deeds save; he said faith saves.

That's why he told us that faith without action is a dead faith. Dead faith is nonexistent faith, although the person holding on to it claims that his faith *is* alive. You may have met people like that. They make all sorts of claims about their faith in God, but nothing in their lives show any evidence of a faith connection with God. Living faith is real. And living faith gives "vital signs" that evidence its existing life. Vital signs for physical life include things like breathing, heartbeat, and brain-wave activity. Vital signs for living faith include obedience to God.

Vital signs are important, but they aren't equal to the living being who manifests them. My heartbeat isn't me; it's a tool used by me to stay alive. And your breathing isn't you; it's a tool you use to breathe. In the same way, works aren't faith; they are the tool faith uses to keep itself alive.

God doesn't confuse me with my heartbeat, and He doesn't confuse your obedience with your faith.

To prove his point James referred to Abraham—the same man Paul said was saved by his faith rather than his obedience.[20] Did James contradict Paul? Not a chance. He used a different story from Abraham's life—James's story was about Abraham sacrificing his son Isaac; Paul's was about circumcision—but his conclusion is the same. First James noted what Abraham *did,* "Was not our ancestor Abraham considered righteous for what he did when he offered his son Isaac on the altar?"[21] Then he pointed out that Abraham's action didn't save him through some kind of law/works setup. His actions proved the existence of his faith, "You see that his faith and his actions were working together, and his faith was made complete by what he did."[22]

His obedience "finished" his faith. Made it complete. Proved it real. Evidenced it alive. But it wasn't his obedience that saved him; James says so in the very next verse. "And the scripture was fulfilled that says, 'Abraham believed God, and it was credited to him as righteousness,' and he was called God's friend."[23] God counted him as righteous because of his faith. If his obedience had earned him righteousness (as law/works would demand), then his righteousness wouldn't be "credited" (NIV) or "imputed" (KJV) to him by God; it would be his by right.

Isn't it interesting that Paul in Romans 4 referenced that same prophecy about Abraham—his faith being credited as righteousness—and then applied it to us? "The words 'it was credited to him' were written not for him alone, but also for us, to whom God will credit righteousness—for us who believe in him who raised Jesus our Lord from the dead."[24] Abraham was saved because he had living faith. So shall we be saved.

In this context James asserts, "You see that a person is justified by what he does and not by faith alone."[25] Read it in context, and it says that we are saved by grace through faith and *not* by the works we do. *But the faith must be alive!*

How does God know it's alive? By looking in our hearts as He looked into Abraham's heart before he was circumcised. How do I know if my faith is alive? By seeing if it evidences the vital signs of life! As John says, "We know that we have come to know him if we obey his commands." God knows before we obey, just as He did with Abraham. We know when we obey. It proves to us that our faith is real.

We're saved when we obey wonderfully well, and we're saved when we fall foolishly flat. Some days your faith may have the strength of a lion. On other days it may demonstrate the weakness of a twenty-year-old overweight Pekingese. But on each of those days, it is still alive. The Bible speaks of great faith, mountain-moving faith, little faith, and weak faith. The great news is that as long as its living faith—no matter how weak or strong—we're saved by the grace of God!

ASSURANCE #4: LOVING FAITH KEEPS YOU IN THE LIGHT

Taking up the theme of salvation in the light, John wrote, "Whoever loves his brother lives in the light, and there is nothing in him to make him stumble."[26] In chapter 1 he wrote that being in the light means that we are constantly being purified. He expanded that here by saying that being in the light means there is nothing in us to make us stumble. *Nothing* to trap us or make us fall.

Being in the light is a wonderful place to be.

To reassure us, he told us there is a sign that we are in the light—a sign that we are saved. Did you see it? We live in the light when we love our brothers. *Live* in the light! That's more than just a visit, an occasional dropping in. It's *living* in a saved relationship with God!

Of course, that reassurance might not bring such peace to you if you doubt that you love your brothers. It seems that John knew some Christians would worry that they don't.

"But how," the worrier asks, "do I know if I really love my brothers? After all, there are some of them I don't even like! And there are days when . . . "

In answer to the anticipated question, the Spirit wrote through John,

> This is how we know what love is: Jesus Christ laid down his life for us. And we ought to lay down our lives for our brothers. If anyone has material possessions and sees his brother in need but has no pity on him, how can the love

of God be in him? Dear children, let us not love with words or tongue but with actions and in truth.[27]

John said the same thing James said, although he approached it differently because of the Gnostic problem. They both taught that saving faith demonstrates itself. It shows signs of life! Living faith doesn't just talk about what a brother needs; living faith provides it for him. If you respond to the needs of brothers and sisters, you respond in love.

And if you respond in love, you live in the light.

Even if your "loving" response is something you don't want to do.

Even if you don't like the people you do it for.

The example John gives of love is that of Jesus going to the cross. He says Jesus' action teaches us what love is. But you and I know that Jesus *didn't want to go!* He begged, "My Father, if it is possible, may this cup be taken from me. Yet not as I will, but as you will."[28] The greatest act of love ever shown wasn't accompanied by overwhelming emotions of warmth and compassion; it was doing the right thing because the Father demanded it. It was wanting to be anywhere but there doing anything but that. Love more clearly shows itself when it acts *against* a person's emotions than in response to them.

Do some Christians with living faith occasionally ignore the needs of others? Of course. Even the apostles once wanted people just to go away so they wouldn't have to find some way to feed them.[29] One time they even wanted people to get their children away from Jesus, apparently seeing them as hindrances rather than people with needs too.[30] Jesus didn't kick Peter, James, John, and the rest out for their demonstrations of lovelessness. He didn't say, "That's it. You guys are just too selfish to be My disciples. Get out of here now! I'll get a bunch who does everything I tell them every

time I tell them." He knew their hearts, knew their predisposi-
tions, and knew their weaknesses. But Jesus didn't equate weakness
with a bad heart lacking faith. He gave mercy and grace.

Even to His own imperfect apostles.

And to you.

As with everything else, He looks for *direction* not *perfection.*
When He told us that loving others means that we are in the light,
He couldn't have meant perfect love. No Christian spends a life-
time perfectly loving our brothers and sisters.

He wants you to obey. He wants you to love. He wants you to
walk in the light, not recline there as if it were your right. He wants
you to avoid sin and seek righteousness. But if in your heart He
sees living faith, He will save you without perfection in any of
these areas. He saves you in spite of your disobedience. He saves
you by His grace through your faith.

You should take comfort in that. He saves you because you have
living faith. He tells you that you can know your faith is alive by
what you do.

Not perfection, direction.

He also tells you what you should do if you doubt your relationship with Him.

Assurance #5: Your Hearts Are Set at Rest

Do you think some of our brothers and sisters in the first century suffered some of the same doubts we do? Struggled with their
own sinfulness? Sometimes didn't like the people they were commanded to love? Vacillated between periods of weak faith and
strong faith?

Sure they did. People are people. Whatever the culture, whatever the era, certain similarities exist among us all.

To those in his day who doubted, John wrote, "This then is how we know that we belong to the truth, and how we set our hearts at rest in his presence whenever our hearts condemn us. For God is greater than our hearts, and he knows everything."[31]

The "this then" in that sentence refers to what he'd just written about loving our brothers in action rather than words. John taught us that our actions of love, which prove to us that we have living faith as described in James 2, should rest our hearts.

Rest our hearts?

Yes. Whenever our hearts condemn us. That's what he said, and that's what he meant.

You know from previous chapters that the heart is where our intellect and emotions come together. It serves as our center of reasoning. When Christians have hurting spirits because they struggle with some sin . . . or refuse to do something they know their Father commands them to do . . . their hearts hurt. Their emotions tell them they have offended God. Legal guilt exists in their intellect; personal guilt exists in their hearts. God's people feel that sensitivity to their own sin, either unintentional or willful, as soon as they recognize the sin.

My daughter Kimberly felt it just the other day. She's only eight but she started thinking about how God must feel about her strong will and her failed efforts to "be good" and obey Mom and Dad. She came to stand beside me as I waited at the back of the church building after preaching one morning. As she stood holding my hand, she started to cry. Gently leading her into the foyer, I sat her down and asked her why she was crying.

"Your sermon was so sad," she said.

"That wasn't a sad sermon," I replied. "It was a happy sermon about how God takes people to heaven because they have living faith."

"I know," she moaned, "but I don't think God will take me to heaven."

"Why?" I queried.

She didn't say anything. She just looked at me with those eyes that said *I'm your child most like you. I don't have to tell you what I feel; you know.*

And I did know.

"Is it because you try so hard to be good but sometimes still disobey Mom and me?"

She bobbed her head yes.

I reassured her of the love of God and the wonders of heaven. I pointed out to her that I love her for wanting to obey perfectly but love her just as much when she fails. I encouraged her to keep the same desire and sensitivity all her life—not toward me but toward her other Father, the one who loves her more than I.

"I don't understand how anyone can love you more than I love you, but God does. He loves you and wants you with Him. Don't worry about Him looking for ways to keep you out of heaven. He's looking for ways to get you in!"

I hurt with her, but I was so happy to see her hurt. That kind of sensitivity shows her good heart, and that's all I can ask of any of my daughters: Have a good heart. It's the key to spiritual life.

This sensitivity to sin and failure to obey should exist in us all. But spiritual sensitivity shouldn't lead us to despair; it should lead us to act. To obey as best we can. To obey in the knowledge that we'll never be good enough, but that's okay. To obey out of gratitude and love to a God who saves us because of our faith.

That's real joy!

So whenever your heart condemns you, remember what God wrote through John, "God is greater than our hearts, and he knows everything." Trust what He says.

ASSURANCE #6: HIS SPIRIT LIVES IN YOU

God isn't just above, around, and beside us. He's also in us in the form of His Holy Spirit. Our obedience and service to Him show us that our faith is alive. They prove to us God's relationship with us. But God also does something to show us our relationship; He places His Spirit in us, alongside our spirits. "We know that we live in him and he in us, because he has given us of his Spirit."[32]

God placed His Spirit in us, His children, as a *guarantee of our salvation.* He "set his seal of ownership on us, and put his Spirit in our hearts as a deposit, guaranteeing what is to come."[33] Yes, that's true of you just as it is for every child of God, "Having believed, you were marked in him with a seal, the promised Holy Spirit, who is a deposit guaranteeing our inheritance."[34]

Believe that too.

And as you discover the blessings of the Spirit of God in your life, thank God for your salvation. Your works show you that you have faith in Him; His indwelling Spirit shows you He keeps faith with you.

ASSURANCE #7: GOD'S LOVE FOR YOU ERADICATES FEAR

If you have taken the assurances in this chapter to heart, you now have confidence that your faith is alive, that God's Spirit is within you, and that God saves you—not because of what *you* do but because of what *He* does in answer to your living faith. Understanding this, you must know that He loves you and blesses you in spite of your imperfections.

The stranger on the bed next to mine in that hospital was not a stranger to God. He was one of God's children. And just as you don't want your children living in terror of you, God doesn't want

His children living in terror of Him. Not the brother facing potential death in the morning. Not the sister facing a lifetime ahead of
her. Not any of us at any time.

That's why Jesus told that prodigal son story. It's why He ate
with prostitutes and other social undesirables. It's why He told the
"town sinner" at Simon the Pharisee's dinner party that she was
forgiven without her so much as saying a word to Him.[35]

God wants us to love Him and desire Him, not live in terror of
Him. He wants us to look forward to death and judgment. As God
told us through John, when we have a living relationship with
Him, "We will have confidence on the day of judgment, because
in this world we are like him. There is no fear in love. But perfect
love drives out fear, because fear has to do with punishment. The
one who fears is not made perfect in love."[36]

Don't let the word *perfect* throw you. God's not looking for
human perfection in love. He's saying that if you still fear Him,
even though you are His, your love isn't yet mature or complete.
That's what the word *perfect* means here. God isn't saying your
unfounded fear is proof of your lack of love or your lack of relationship with Him. His point is that you should keep growing. He
wants you to reach the level of communication and understanding
with Him so that you no longer live in terror of facing Him.

He loves you.

He's looking forward to being with you through eternity.

And He wants you to know that.

ASSURANCE #8: GOD HEARS OUR PRAYERS

To make sure we understand just how wonderful this relationship is, John told us that the benefits are more than just overcoming fear. Because we are God's children, He *treats* us like His

children. Yes, He'll treat us like children in heaven, but more than that. Here. On earth.

Just after telling us that he wrote the letter "so that you may know that you have eternal life," John wrote, "This is the confidence we have in approaching God: that if we ask anything according to his will, he hears us. And if we know that he hears us—whatever we ask—we know that we have what we asked of him."[37]

God in heaven sees your imperfect, vacillating faith that leads you to the peaks of spiritual highs and the valleys of spiritual lows. The wonderful news of grace is that He blesses you not only on the mountains but also in the canyons. Even weak faith, because it is alive, receives the blessings of God—including His answering your prayers.

James made that point powerfully in the last chapter of his book. He referred to Elijah, "a man just like us,"[38] as proof that God answers prayer. Elijah moved to the spiritual summit when he killed the prophets of Baal.[39] But he quickly fell into the spiritual pits when Jezebel threatened his life. He ran and hid like some coward rather than a representative of God.[40] When James described him as a person like us, he hit the nail squarely. Yet God answered Elijah's prayers. He answers yours too—victor or coward—with the same faithfulness He answered Elijah's.[41]

You know God wouldn't answer you if He found you displeasing. Or repulsive. Or lost. The fact that He answers you serves as another proof of your saved relationship with Him.

So go ahead. Try it. (Especially if your personal guilt caused you to quit praying as you should.) Ask Him for something.

No, not a Mercedes in the driveway. Silly, selfish requests don't get answered the way you wish.[42] Ask Him to speak to your heart, telling you that you shouldn't believe your doubts, but His word. Ask Him to move His Spirit within you so that you will see Him in action in the next few days—guiding, protecting, or comforting. Don't ask Him for a sign of His deity;[43] ask Him to show you what He wants of you.[44]

Seriously.

I'm honestly challenging you to ask God to act. You have every right; you are His child. He has every wish to convince you that you are. Don't set any boundaries on Him. Ask Him to do it His way, but ask Him to open your eyes so that when He answers the prayer, you will have the spiritual wisdom to know He acted.

He wants you to know you are saved.

And He wants to answer your prayers. "We know that we have what we asked of him." Ask Him now.

Ask Him to spiritually heal you.

Not only is He not going to send
you to hell, He'll give you heaven.

෴

Therefore, there is now no condemnation for
those who are in Christ Jesus.

Romans 8:1

CHAPTER 9

Answer Satan's Lies
with God's Truth

No other event in my life touches the mind-stopping, body-draining terror I felt the night the clouds caught fire. My heart froze in mid-beat as my lungs abandoned their quest for air, as my mind forgot all other functions but its effort to focus exclusively on the destruction sweeping rapidly toward me. I helplessly watched the sign of God flash through the skies.

I wasn't ready to meet Him.

It happened late one night in the 1970s when Alice and I were still in our early twenties, a time in our life when we knew considerably less about God than we do now. We'd visited her parents in Tallassee, Alabama, for a couple of days, and lingered a bit too long on Saturday evening before heading home to LaGrange, Georgia, where I was to preach the next day. We crammed the car with our baby's equipage, hugged and waved our good-byes, and started on the two-hour trip that had become routine to us. For several miles we worked our way from one deserted country lane to another in a crooked and lonely path to Interstate 85, the concrete expanse that would speed our journey. As we drove, I noted a bank of clouds gathering in the distance to the south of us, but was not alarmed—that was a typical sight in a normal night of driving the back roads of rural Alabama. I casually returned to mentally practicing my sermon while Alice sang to our toddler, Angela.

All that would change in a moment, in the twinkling of an eye.

Making our last turn to the south to reach the Interstate and coming out from under a canopy of trees, we topped a hill just in time to see a rainbow streak of light explode across the horizon ahead of us. At least a third of the heavens within our view glowed in strange and magnificent colors.

It truly looked as if the clouds were on fire.

"Joe!" It was the only thing Alice said, fear strangling any other words that tried to escape. I glanced over and saw her clutching Angela tightly and staring with panicked eyes through the windshield. She wanted me to explain, give an answer, reassure.

But I couldn't. I was paralyzed by the thought that Jesus had returned. In a moment we would see Him and see fiery angels darting around and beyond Him, swooping to the earth to capture and, in flaming fire, "take vengeance" on the evil.[1]

I knew they were coming for me.

There was nothing I could do.

It was too late.

I could see the Interstate just ahead now, but it offered no avenue of escape. Even though I preached for Him and loved Him, I hadn't found victory over my sinful desires nor had I done all I knew to do. I felt staggering horror that I would be weighed in the balance and found wanting. I knew I would hear, "Throw him into 'the lake which burneth with fire and brimstone.' "[2]

It never occurred to me to stop the car or to turn around and drive back toward Tallassee. I drove toward the cloud in mindless terror, expecting to be snatched away from my godly wife and innocent child at any moment.

Terrible thought for a Christian, isn't it?

To understand why I reacted as I did, you have to realize that I spent the first few years of my Christian life tormented by the great fear that I would not make it to heaven because of my continuing weaknesses. If ever there was a Christian who was guilt-caged, it was I.

Obviously, the phenomenon we experienced that night wasn't the coming of Judgment Day. The next day we heard an ambiguous report about some sort of military missile going awry and exploding, frightening people in parts of Alabama, Georgia, and Florida.

It definitely frightened at least two.

Since that time I've learned not to live in that kind of fear, dreading to meet my Father. I've learned that God wants me to be secure in my relationship with Him. I've learned that I will always, no matter where I am in my spiritual walk, be weighed by the scales of almighty God and found wanting. But one thing makes all the difference—God's grace is greater than my sin. I no longer fear Jesus' coming. Rather, I long for it. Not because I've reached some mystical level of personal holiness, but because I am secure in the belief that I am God's forgiven child.

THE DIFFICULTY OF BELIEVING IT'S FOR US

God wants you to be secure in that belief too. But Satan and his demons have other plans. They remind you of your sin; they focus your attention on you and what you've done wrong. They know that when you're focused on your own shortcomings and fears, you cannot be focused on the cross of Christ.

Let me share with you five lies that Satan uses to distract you from the cross and the forgiveness bought by the blood of Christ. Along with those lies, I will share with you God's truth so that you can combat Satan when he attempts to sabotage your faith.

LIE #1: "YOU DON'T DESERVE TO BE FORGIVEN"

Remember the story of Rick in chapter 1? His path to spiritual healing was blockaded because he knew better than to commit the sins with which he struggled. Raised in a good Christian home, educated in a religious school, and befriended by people serving Jesus, he couldn't blame his sin on ignorance. And because he knew better but committed the sin anyway, he convinced himself that he didn't deserve the forgiveness of God.

In a very real way, Rick felt just like the prodigal son: "Father, I have sinned against heaven and against you. I am no longer worthy to be called your son."[3]

Maybe you, too, feel there is no way you deserve the forgiveness of God. You knew better than to do whatever it is that you feel so guilty about. Maybe you taught a Bible class. Perhaps you're a church leader, a minister, a professor at a Bible college or seminary, or a respected member of your church. Or perhaps you've gone to church all your life. You knew what was right, yet you did what was wrong. You know in your heart that you do not deserve the mercy and grace of God. Like the prodigal son, you'd settle for mercy. Yet you haven't the nerve to ask for grace.

Christopher couldn't. Many times in church I'd been touched in the inner recesses of my soul by his eloquent and fervent supplications to God. A prayer warrior, if there has ever been one. But when he faced the personal guilt of his terrible sin, he quit praying altogether.

His sin fell into a category that turned many who had once looked to him for shepherding into indignant Christians who didn't want to see him again. He couldn't agree with that sentiment more. He felt that all he deserved was the condemnation and ostracization of God and His people.

To prove to me that he didn't deserve either mercy or grace, he said, "Joe, I led her to Jesus. Then I led her to my bed. How could any man find such a wonderful person, show her and her husband the way to Jesus, witness the miracle of her conversion, and have an affair with her within months of her salvation?

"No good man could do that. Certainly not a Christian man. She may walk away from everything spiritual for the rest of her life, and I will have been the cause.

"I don't deserve God's forgiveness. Don't you agree?"

I replied, "Christopher, you're right. You don't deserve the forgiveness of God."

Surprised by my answer? You shouldn't be. He didn't deserve God's mercy or grace. Neither do I. And neither do you.

TRUTH #1: YOU DON'T DESERVE IT!

I have news for you. News from God. No one deserves God's mercy! But the great news of God is that the mercy and grace of God aren't offered to those who deserve it. They are offered to those who, in brokenness before God, place their faith in Him. That's why Jesus died.

"Christ died for the ungodly."[4]

"God demonstrates his own love for us in this: While we were still sinners, Christ died for us."[5]

When you pray, tell God you don't deserve His mercy and grace. It's okay. In Jesus' story of the prodigal, that's what the boy did. But know that God's response, as told by Jesus, was that He'll interrupt your sorrowful soliloquy with manifestations not only of His mercy but also of His grace. Not only is He *not* going to send you to hell,

He'll give you heaven. Quit thinking about how bad you've been and start praising Him for how good He is. His goodness is so far beyond any and all of your badness that He loves you and wants to forgive you anyway—even though you don't deserve it.

That's what I told Christopher. I could say it with authority because that's what God tells all of us. Christopher can't change what he did, nor can he have the influence on his young convert/lover that he could have had. But he has one thing without doubt. The mercy and grace of God. God forgave him without stopping to consider for a moment whether he deserved it or not.

Believe it because God said it.

LIE #2: "YOUR SIN IS TOO BAD"

In the late 1970s, Dennis Randall and I conducted a live call-in radio program on WGBF in Evansville, Indiana, every Sunday morning. People called in their Bible questions, and we did our best to answer them using the Bibles and reference tools sprawled on the table between us. Most questions weren't too hard, theologically speaking, but some would break our hearts. Like the lady who called one morning with a shy voice that made us press our earphones tight to hear her.

"Please, sir, will God forgive a person who's killed someone?"

Something in her voice told me this wasn't a Sunday school question.

"Ma'am, did you kill someone?" I asked quietly, gently.

"Yes."

Even with that single word, there was something in her voice.

"Ma'am, did you murder that person?"

"Yes."

Dennis and I stared at each other, each trying to decide what to say next. But she spoke again. Slowly. Painfully.

"In 1959 I murdered a man. I went to prison and served time. Not long ago I got out of prison, and I've gone to church after church in this town asking ministers if God will forgive a murderer. Every one so far has told me no, God doesn't forgive murderers.

"Please, sir, can God ever forgive me?"

If you had been sitting there with me, what would you have told her? Was her sin too evil to forgive?

TRUTH #2: GRACE INCREASES IN PROPORTION TO THE SIN

I opened my Bible to Romans 5 and read verse 20 to her, "Where sin increased, grace increased all the more."[6] I then led her through the teachings of that great chapter to show her that the atonement of Jesus overcomes even the greatest of sins.

Even murder.

Or adultery.

Or homosexual prostitution.

Or anything else.

God demonstrated that degree of mercy and grace with King David. David committed adultery with Bathsheba, then ordered the murder of her husband Uriah—two heinous sins. Yet even as David admitted, "I have sinned against the Lord," God in mercy replied through Nathan, "The Lord has taken away your sin. You are not going to die."[7]

If you've killed, fornicated, stolen, or slandered, God can and will forgive you. There is no sin beyond the reaches of His mercy and grace.

You may have to face some temporal consequences of your sin—as Rick did when he contracted AIDS and King David did through the seeds of sin sown in his children—but God will completely remove the sin and all its eternal consequences.

So if you fear facing God because of what you've done, here's your defense strategy come Judgment Day. Look right into God's eyes when you stand before His throne and say, "I take the fifth."

No, not the Fifth Amendment to the U.S. Constitution. God isn't bound by that law.

The fifth chapter of Romans.

Tell Him you believed Him when He said His grace is bigger than any sin. Even the sin you've done.

LIE #3: "BECAUSE YOU STILL WANT TO SIN, YOU HAVE NO HOPE"

I honestly don't know where we ever got the idea that faithful penitence means that the desire for sin will simply disappear. I know it wasn't from God. Remember in Romans 6 where we saw that God's crucifying of our past (our old self) didn't kill our sinful nature? Christians still make choices about whether to sin or not to sin.

A couple of years ago a lady came to me at the conclusion of a revival service where I'd spoken. Pulling me aside so that no one could hear, she asked me if a person who had lived in a sin for a period of time would mourn the sin once it was abandoned. She was a visitor to our revival that night. Came because of an advertisement she'd run across. As God would have it, I preached on Satan's attacks and God's victories. Of course, I described temptation and sin rather graphically, since unfortunately, I know so much about it. I also described mercy and grace graphically, since fortunately, I know something about that too. God took those words and used them to penetrate the woman's heart. She saw her sin, she faced her God, and she realized what she must do.

There was only one problem. She wondered whether she would grieve over the sin once she gave it up for God. I'd never thought about it in those terms, but her question created an instant "aha!" in my mind. It gave me a way to understand and explain a concept I knew but had never articulated well.

If my flesh—my sinful nature—finds itself strongly tempted by some sin, it doesn't lose its appetite for that sin just because the Spirit of God influences my mind to make a decision to walk away.

I've talked to Christians escaping sin who loved how it felt, loved what it gave them, or loved the person who partnered in the sin with them. Perhaps the clearest example is to think in terms of an affair—a man grieves for the lover he left to be right with Jesus. His grief doesn't mean he's unforgiven. It means he's human. Humans grieve over the loss of a love—even a forbidden love. We're made that way. Any sin that seemed to fill some need will have the same effect. A person abandoning it will miss the sin and mourn it.

A young girl escaping a satanic cult spent the better part of an hour telling me how afraid of Satan she was. She'd seen things she believed to be murder, infanticide, and worse. For more than a decade, from her fifth year of life through her fifteenth, she served Satan through active membership in the cult. Some of the things they used her for frightened me just to hear. Finally, in desperation, she sought help and had been moved by authorities to a home in another city. When I asked why she trembled so, now that she was safe, she replied that she wasn't sure if she would ever be safe from the reach of Satan. Then, almost in total contradiction to her fear, she said, "But I love him." Had it not been for the woman asking me months earlier about grieving abandoned sin, I'm not sure I would have understood the emotional contradiction. Now it made sense. No matter how much a person may hate the sin or the consequence, there was something in it that seemed to meet some need. At the very least, it was familiar, comfortable. Even a person fleeing Satan missed him and mourned the loss of the relationship.

In the same way, an addict to pornography may grieve over the magazines he burned in the backyard. A drunkard may grieve the loss of the numbness she felt when drunk. The drug addict grieves the missing high.

Yes, there is often grief from abandoned sin.

Similar to the grief of losing a loved one to death, though not usually as intense.

It's a natural occurance. Human beings can become so attached to particular sins that they mourn losing what it did for them.

TRUTH #3: GRIEF OVER ABANDONED SIN DOESN'T MEAN GOD HASN'T FORGIVEN YOU

Mourning abandoned sin doesn't mean you are still the same old person that did the sin. When you turned to God in living faith, He made you brand-new.

Believe that.

But He didn't erase your memory bank or surgically remove your emotions. He didn't blank out your past so that you have no connection with it in your mind ever again. He left you as you— only not the *same* you. He made you new. And even though you still remember who you were, you are no longer the same. Because you retain the memory, you may retain the emotions that go with it. Don't be afraid of that.

After Alice and I had been remarried for a couple of years, she asked the question that I figured must eventually come. She said, "Do you ever miss it? Do you ever find yourself thinking about the things you did and wanting to go back to them?"

If she'd asked such a penetrating question in our first marriage, I likely would have lied. Not in this marriage; this one is based on honesty and openness. So, I told her truthfully, "Yes. Some days I find myself thinking about some of the things I did and wishing I could do them again right now. I miss some things. Terribly. But I don't feel that way often, and as time passes, I feel it less intensely when the thoughts do come."

"If a part of you wants to do them, why don't you?"

"It's simple, baby. I want you more than I want that. I'll never leave God, you, or my children again. A passing memory and a fleeting desire don't compare to you."

My answer satisfied Alice. Maybe it's even more important that it satisfied me. It kept me from doubting my own sincerity or commitment whenever those feelings occasionally smuggled themselves into my mind.

Missing or wanting the sin doesn't mean you're evil to the core.

"Falling off the wagon" and slipping into the sin again doesn't either. If that happens, don't wallow in it. Leave the sin again, knowing now how Satan will use your emotions against you.

Of course, by telling you not to let a momentary lapse of sin throw you, I don't mean that the sin is inconsequential. Nor do I mean to imply that random slipping should be the norm. I believe quite strongly that the healing power of God can remove the power of the temptation over you. At the same time, many good Christians trying to obey God do find that the path to healing isn't instantaneous. Sometimes the path is littered with traps and lures. Avoid them with all your heart, but if you believe that a lapse or two proves you inadequate, some kind of spiritual fraud, then satanic forces will pull out all stops to get you into those sad situations. Don't believe them. Don't let the fact that you struggle make you believe that God hasn't forgiven or that you're evil at heart.

If you believe the demonic lies that say your desire, grief, or momentary setback shows you are "hopeless," you will open yourself for the sin to control you again. It will wrap itself around you until it rules you and destroys your faith.

So don't believe demons when they tell you you are hopeless. Your grief or desire doesn't mean you're hopeless; it means you're human.

Don't believe Satan's lies about you. Believe what God tells you about your wholeness.

LIE #4: "YOU'RE NOT FORGIVEN BECAUSE SOME PEOPLE HAVEN'T FORGIVEN YOU"

It's true that God wants you to seek forgiveness from those you've offended. Jesus said, "If you are offering your gift at the altar and there remember that your brother has something against you, leave your gift there in front of the altar. First go and be reconciled to your brother; then come and offer your gift."[8] But you'll have to accept the fact that fallible humans often won't do what God tells them to do. All you can do is ask their forgiveness; you cannot force them to forgive you.

Jesus told a story about an unforgiving brother that might help you recognize Satan's lies. This guy's younger brother had left home some time earlier and had spent all his father's hard-earned money on parties and the wrong people. You may be more familiar with the younger brother—the prodigal son.[9] But for this discussion, let's look at the older brother. As you deal with your sin, it's likely that you'll encounter a few of these guys.

The older brother was an obedient son. While his younger brother had run wild, he'd stayed home "slaving for his dad." When the prodigal returned, his father gave mercy and grace. Total forgiveness *and* a party. The older brother saw his father's extravagant forgiveness as unfair and ungodly. Clearly, he followed the law/works system of salvation! In essence, the older brother shouted, "You can't give him any good thing until he earns it—just like I did! Make him pay! *If* we ever take him back and forgive him, he *must* do something more than show up. He must not only satisfy you, he must also satisfy *me,* because I deserve that right! It wasn't just you he sinned against; he also sinned against me!"

But God, operating under a grace/faith system, doesn't think like that. In this story, Jesus shows that He reserves the right to give more to the returning sinner than to the slaving saint, if He so chooses.

Why would God do that?

Because the grace/faith system rewards faith, not works.

Some long-suffering church people don't like grace given to sinners with living faith. They don't like the idea of God rewarding faith rather than the accumulated good deeds of a lifetime. Yet they can't get mad at God for doing it; that would violate the law. So they get mad at the people God forgives. They attack them instead of the God who won't operate by their rules.

I can give too many examples of Christians who have committed some "major league" sin and then tried to make that sin right by telling individuals or a whole church how penitent they are, only to be treated with contempt and disdain. I've experienced it myself. I use myself as an example because I want you to know how God works things out. After the sinful period of my life that I told you about in the book's beginning, I did everything humanly possible to gain the forgiveness of my brethren. But not all forgive. For example, several years ago a leader in a church in the northern part of a large metropolitan area near where I live told a group of people lobbying to have me considered for a ministry position there, "You know Joe's past. There are just some things you can't get beyond." A church in the southern part of that same city put out the word that it considered me unworthy to preach. "He's a known sinner," some pointed out.

Just this past spring I was invited by a major university to tell "my story" of sin and subsequent forgiveness. At the conclusion, a Christian wrote the university, "A man like Joe should not be in a leadership position in the church."

No, don't pity me. I don't pity myself. I know I'm forgiven; I have both mercy and grace. I can't begin to tell you all the blessings God has given—and is giving—to this undeserving sinner. I only tell you what happened to me so you can see two things. The first is that you aren't alone. All us "known sinners" have people who remind us of our forgiven sin and will for the rest of our lives. But we must remember that God ignores their condemnation and wants us to do the same. He uses "known sinners" in His work and blesses them mightily.

I left my sin and guilt with God. If some brothers or sisters want to help Him share my load of shed sin, that's their business. They can carry it in their hearts if they choose. I'm forgiven. I refuse to carry it in mine.

I believe the badge sent me by Ron Pope, a brother in Christ. Often I pin it on and wear it happily. It says:

Joe Beam
Known sinner
Saved by grace

I am, you know. And so are you, if you have living faith in the Lord Jesus.

God gives me opportunities to speak in revivals in far-flung places of the globe. You may wish to check the pages at the end of this book for topics that may be of value to your church. Every year I speak for thirty or more Christian events, some lasting several days. Thousands of people attend the revivals that churches graciously invite me to conduct. The nonprofit corporation I founded and head, Family Dynamics Institute, works with several thousand families each year—strengthening and, sometimes, saving them. If God can use a "known sinner" like me, then He certainly will use a "known sinner" like you.

Even if some Christians resent His doing so.

If you encounter some of these unforgiving "older brothers" in your quest for spiritual healing, remember the other part of the story.

When the sinful son finally came to his senses, he mournfully headed home. He fully intended to throw himself on his father's mercy and beg that he not be given the rejection he deserved, but that he be allowed to work on his father's farm as a hired hand— at least then he would be able to eat. But the boy underestimated his father's love—just as many of us do.

His father had been waiting for him.

Truth #4: God Throws a Party in Heaven When a Prodigal Returns

Every day, the father would stand at the end of the road, strain his eyes, and look as far as he could, hoping to see a speck on the horizon that would be his son. And on the day the boy climbed that last hill toward home, his father was at the end of the road . . . waiting. And when he saw his son, the father *ran* to meet him. He would hear nothing of his working among the hired hands! He called for his servants to bring a robe and a ring and told them to prepare the fatted calf he had been saving for such a special occasion. Instead of merely giving the boy the mercy he hoped for, he extended lavish grace! Instead of the rejection the older son thought appropriate, the father threw the wayward son a party!

And that's what happens in heaven when you repent. The Father throws a party in your honor.

My dear friends, Clay and Debbie Humphries, are returned prodigals also. A few years ago they each sinned against the other and lost the ministry God had given them. By the grace of God, Clay now preaches again and Debbie has a unique ministry to hurting women. Every once in a while, someone throws Clay's seven-years-forgiven sin into his face with a self-righteous sneer. I usually know when they do it, because that's when Clay calls with that same opening line, "Now, Joe, tell me again about that party in heaven they had for Debbie and me."

We lament, laugh, and remind each other of the forgiveness of God. Even the angels liked it that God forgave—they got to have a party when it happened! Heaven forgave us, even if some people never can.

God's forgiveness of you isn't predicated on the forgiveness of others—even those you've sinned against. God doesn't ask unforgiving Christians for references about you. He looks in your heart and decides for Himself.

If you choose to accept people's snubs, comments, and lifted noses as proof of your lack of forgiveness, you obviously have that option. But just because you believe those people doesn't mean God does.

He believes in you.

You'll be healed when you believe Him in return.

LIE #5. GOD MAY LOVE OTHERS, BUT NOT YOU

Sensitive Christians, who are deeply aware of their sin, sometimes can't believe that God's love is for them. He may love others—people whose sin is not as bad as theirs—but there is no way God could love them.

Such people often see God as a vengeful, angry father who is ever ready to pounce on them in judgment. These same people often view any difficulty that comes into their lives as evidence that they must have done something to anger God. They see their relationship with God as tenuous, always on the verge of breaking.

Not too long ago, I sat in a meeting room in a women's prison and listened to the prayer requests of the inmates. For several minutes I jotted them down, making sure I got the details right. Finally, just before I prayed, I noticed something. Not one of them had asked me to pray for herself. All the requests were for someone else—a brother, husband, child, or mother.

When I asked the valiant Christian workers who had invited me, they explained. "These ladies don't believe God loves them. For most of them, no man in their lives ever has. They see men—even fathers—as wanting something from them and believe their value and worth come only from their ability to provide it. They asked you to pray because they think God doesn't view them as important. You've now met people who truly believe they are unlovable."

It broke my heart to discover they didn't think God loved them. Not too long afterward, I shared the story in a Bible class. Within the next few days, I heard from several people in that class—good, active Christians—who believed the same thing about themselves. No, not to the extreme of the women I met in prison. But enough to make my heart break all over again.

TRUTH #5: GOD LOVED YOU ENOUGH TO GIVE HIS INNOCENT CHILD

Often, the reason such Christians can't believe God's love is for them is that they don't understand the extent of God's love. If you have a hard time believing that God could love you, perhaps this analogy will help.

Suppose one of your children committed a capital crime and sat on death row awaiting execution. In your love for that child, you searched for any and every legal ground or loophole to rescue him from such a horrible end. You see his sorrow. You know his pain. You know he deserves death because there is no question that he committed the crime. When he gets angry, he screams at you that he will do it again if he gets the chance. But at other times, when he isn't agitated, he tells you he's sorry and is filled with regret. Your friends and neighbors tell you it's not your fault; he's just no good. They can't understand why you would continue to involve yourself with someone like him, even if he is your son. And your son, the criminal, can't understand it either.

You can't explain it any other way than to say that it's not what he's done but your love that drives your care, your desire to free him from the fate he made for himself.

How far would you go to show your wayward son your love, to save his life? Would you die in his stead? That's noble. But would you go one step further . . . a cavern-wide leap further?

Let's say your state has a law stating that a death-row inmate may go free, completely and without recrimination, if a blood relative dies in his place. But the law has one catch. The relative who dies must be completely innocent. The relative must be a young child—better yet, a toddler.

Would you give the life of your innocent baby for the life of your criminal son? Could you walk into the prison, give a last loving look at your trusting infant, barely old enough to talk, and then hand the child over to the executioner? Could you sit just outside the room where they strapped that baby to two boards fixed perpendicular to each other, his little arms held out to his side and strapped to the crosspiece while his little legs are tied together to the end of the other board? Could you listen to his screams, his terrified voice calling your name over and over in fear and confusion? Could you watch the executioners laugh at his pathetic attempts to free himself and then callously throw the switch that pulsates stinging, burning, killing electricity through the convulsing little body?

And, then, after it is over, could you walk down the hall to get your other son? Could you put your arms around him, hold him tight, and walk him to his freedom?

If you could, you would understand the nature of God. You are the criminal child—deserving death and guilty as charged. But the truth is that no matter what you've done, God's love is greater than all your sin. Greater than your rebellion, your anger, your evil deeds. He willingly paid the ultimate price—He gave His innocent child in exchange for you.

> You see, at just the right time, when we were still power-less, Christ died for the ungodly. Very rarely will anyone die for a righteous man, though for a good man someone might possibly dare to die. But God demonstrates his own love for us in this: While we were still sinners, Christ died for us.[10]

He died for you while you were still a sinner. The declaration of Romans 8:1 rings loud and clear: "There is now no condemnation for those who are in Christ Jesus"!

As His child, believe the declaration and be *healed*.

When we see that God's children love us, in spite of our sin, we begin to believe that God can love us too.

❧

Therefore confess your sins to each other and pray for each other so that you may be healed. The prayer of a righteous man is powerful and effective.

James 5:16

C H A P T E R

Confess and Be Healed

Bright-red, burnt-gold, and chocolate-brown leaves swirled around us in the autumn breeze, tagging each other and scampering for safety before they could in turn be caught. The older, browner leaves joined just as enthusiastically in the game as the younger, brighter ones, though a bit more noisily. I was glad they felt like playing. I felt like dying.

Just days before, Dr. Daniel Boone had told me that the rapid physical deterioration I was experiencing resulted from guilt buried within me.[1] Dr. Boone could actually feel my bones rubbing together as he placed his hands on my shoulder and asked me to move about. After rigorously testing me for physical causes of my problem, he determined there were none and directed me to find spiritual healing. If I didn't find that healing, he warned me, my spiritual sickness would continue to wreak havoc on my body and mind.

Maybe I should have known that was my problem before I spent so much money on medical tests. I knew I strongly felt a burden of overwhelming guilt for something I'd done a few years before—something I still find dreadful to remember, although the world around me would laugh it off as nothing. I had asked God to forgive me, but somehow I couldn't believe He had. I even reminded myself of the story of Bobby and Jeff,[2] but it made no difference.

As part of my prescription for healing, Daniel told me I needed an understanding Christian to guide me to the healing power of God.

He also told me to pray.

I did both. I prayed for God to send me the understanding Christian who would penetrate the fog in my heart and guide me to His healing power. I prayed that God would heal me.

Walking in the Kentucky woods with my new friend, Jim Leek, on that wonderful fall day turned out to be the answer to my petitions.

I was speaking at a retreat for college students active in a church student center in Lexington, Kentucky. They preferred to leave campus for their annual retreat, so we drove quite a distance into the countryside to a state park where the group had rented rooms for the weekend. Jim Leek had served the church as an elder for years before moving to Albany, Georgia, and had returned to be with the college students during their retreat.

Or at least that's why he thought he was there.

It later became apparent that God had placed him there to bring my spiritual healing to completion. The healing process had begun just days before as Alice drove me to a seminar I was to do for a psychiatric hospital in Nashville. She drove because I had only the strength to lie in the backseat, unable to sit for the six hours it took to reach our destination. As I lay there, I prayed. Well, it was sort of a prayer. Mostly I lamented my condition to God.

"God, I don't know why this is happening to me. Daniel says it's guilt, and I know You don't want me to feel guilty. My mind says You have forgiven me, but my heart just can't believe it. Well, at least one thing has come of this. I've lost everything. If I can't work, we'll go broke in short order. I have nothing to rely on but You. You're all I have left."

Isn't it amazing that stating the obvious can sometimes jar our sensibilities? No sooner had I told God I had nothing left but my *faith in Him* than I remembered a request I made just before my health began to fail. I had asked God to give me more faith, faith free from doubt.

I chuckled at the remembrance—laughed right in the midst of the pain I'd been so carefully hiding from Alice. Looking back over the last few months, things became obvious. I had prayed for faith, and my health insurance was mysteriously cancelled within days. Shortly after that I became sick, and the sickness got worse and worse and worse over several months. Daniel helped me to see that my sickness grew from guilt hidden inside me. Now God, at my request, had brought me to the point where *faith* was all I had left. And that's what He'd been trying to tell me: Faith was all I needed.

The timing of His answer showed God's loving wisdom.

When I committed the sin about which I carried such personal guilt, leaves had swirled around me and a brisk autumn wind chilled the air. God brought me to healing on the anniversary of my abomination. The final step of my healing was set in order.

"Joe," Jim said in his usual quiet voice as he walked and I limped through the forest, "what's eating you?"

I doubt he knew at the time how accurate his phrasing was.

We found an unoccupied cabin and commandeered the rocking chairs already swaying in anticipation of our approach like friendly old hounds welcoming guests to their homeplace. I sat for a while, resting from the effort of the walk and wondering what I could tell Jim. Months before, in our initial acquaintance, I'd tested his views on grace and forgiveness. Maybe I had sensed back then, on some subconscious level, that I would need him someday. He didn't push. He didn't lean in my direction or stare at me with probing eyes. He rocked in his borrowed chair, watched the leaves frolic, and waited for me to decide whether to answer.

"Jim . . . I . . . ah . . . I need to tell you something. It was a few years ago, just about this time of year . . ."

I explained without emotion, telling the whole story without fanfare or slant. I told him things I hadn't told Daniel. Sometimes I'd falter in my narrative, and Jim would ask a clarifying question. He wasn't pushing, just making sure he understood. When I finished my sad tale, I didn't look at him. I didn't want to see any recrimination in his eyes if it were there.

"You know, Joe," he gently explained, "sometimes a person doesn't heal from a sin until he's mourned it. Have you grieved over your sin?"

"Sure I have. I'm truly sorry it happened, and I'll never do anything like it again. Ever!"

"No, I mean more than that. Maybe I should ask it this way: Have you ever cried over that sin?"

"Jim," I patiently educated, "that isn't my nature. Women cry. Men don't. At least, Beam men don't. I'm sorry, and I grieve that it happened, but no, I've never cried over it and don't expect to."

He didn't react to that last statement. He took his time, thought it through, and did a remarkable thing beyond the boundaries of my experience. He placed his hand on my knee, looked me lovingly in the eye, and pronounced, "I forgive you."

In the theological scheme of things, I guess that doesn't make sense. I certainly didn't sin against Jim. He didn't even know me when I committed the heinous sin. It was neither his place nor his right to forgive me.

But none of those thoughts crossed my mind when he said those three words. I couldn't have thought them because I was so amazed by the tears coursing down my cheeks as soon as the sound of his pronouncement reached my ears. Jim's words uncorked the guilt hiding in me, and I became aware of my sinfulness before God like never before. Like the "town sinner" in Luke 7, my pain, shame, and remorse flowed from my heart, through my eyes, and onto someone else's floor.

I sobbed before Jesus while my friend held my hand.

As I sit in my home office writing this story for you, I pause occasionally to contemplate the leaves outside my window. They're the reds, yellows, and browns of a vivid fall. Some have already dived from the trees into our pool, choosing to swim rather than play chase with the others tumbling happily in the backyard breeze. Most haven't fallen yet; they gleefully wait for me to rake the yard so they can float merrily down as soon as I turn my back.

But thanks to God, I *can* rake them. I can even jump into the pool and cavort with the multicolored swimmers, if the water isn't too cold. It's been years since God started my physical healing on a beautiful fall day in Kentucky, and I no longer worry about not being able to work and support my family.

Kimberly will be home from second grade in just a little while, and I've promised her we'll play together when she gets home. Maybe we'll invite some of the leaves to join us.

Oh, my bones creak and ache a little, especially this time of year, but that's age and allergies. The debilitating disease that was hustling me toward being a cripple was healed by God. It came as a direct result of His healing me spiritually.

Isn't it time for you to let Him do the same for you? The final step in the process is *confession*. I've delayed discussing confession until this chapter because the subject is so important to spiritual healing.

What Confession Does Not Do

In earlier chapters, I've pointed out that the saving grace of God isn't predicated on our action; it comes in response to our yielding to God in saving faith. Confession does not serve as a panacea for sin. We shouldn't sin thinking, "Oh, well, as soon as I confess, God will remove the guilt of my sin. I will make the 'payment' of confession, and God will hand over the 'product' of forgiveness." That isn't the way it works.

In one of the strongest biblical teachings demanding confession, John wrote, "If we confess our sins, he is faithful and just and will forgive us our sins and purify us from all unrighteousness."[3] Because of the "if" in that verse, many people think sin is held against us until it is confessed. Approaching this Scripture from a law/works mind-set, that sentence could be seen as a conditional requirement for salvation—sin is only forgiven when we confess it. But a grace/faith approach doesn't see it that way at all.

Let's place that scripture back into its context and see what God is telling us. In verse 7, He tells us that "if" we are in the light, Jesus' blood "purifies" us. Every sin is washed off as it occurs. Now, if your sin is forgiven as soon as it occurs—if you are being purified constantly because you are in the light—then sin isn't charged to your account. God charges it to the account of Jesus. If the sin isn't on your account, how can you be guilty of it until you think to confess it?

No, God doesn't hold each sin against you until you confess it. Because believers are in the light, He *continually* cleanses you from all sin.

Now if that's true, then what did John mean when he said God forgives us "if" we confess? Because John wrote to an area plagued by Gnostic heresies, the book of 1 John battled one Gnostic false teaching after another. The Gnostics believed they didn't sin because their spirits couldn't be held responsible for what their flesh did. When John spoke of our confessing sin, he spoke to the heresy of the Gnostics who thought themselves sinless. If we consider ourselves sinless, we will never move into the aware spiritual state. We will remain in the deceived state, recognizing neither legal nor personal guilt. John said we will never get into the light until we realize that we are sinners and place our faith in Jesus, the same Jesus who came in the flesh. John wasn't teaching that each sin is forgiven only when confessed; he was teaching that we must confess that we are sinners. Only sinners seek salvation in Jesus. Everyone else seeks salvation in themselves.

So don't misconstrue John's teaching to make him contradict himself. He doesn't tell us in verse 7 we are continually cleansed and then in verse 9 that we aren't, that we only have periodic cleansing as we confess each sin. Confession is not a trick or talisman we use to make God forgive us. He forgives us because we are in the light, because we are Christians living by faith in the Son Most High.

WHAT CONFESSION DOES

Christians are forgiven of sins even before they confess them. After all, if I'm saved, I'm forgiven—at least legally forgiven. But we want more than legal forgiveness, don't we? We also want our personal guilt removed. The way to find that spiritual healing is to come to grips with our own sinfulness. Confession allows us to do that.

Several years ago, I met a Christian teenager who was battling a problem that, at the time, I didn't know how to address. She had sneaked out of her house one evening to go to a party her parents had forbidden her to attend. At the party, she drank some beer and smoked a little. When she crawled through her bedroom window shortly before dawn, the light flicked on and there stood both Mom and Dad. They could see she'd gone out against their wishes. They also smelled the alcohol and tobacco on her breath. As you might imagine, quite a scene took place that night, and they placed her on restriction for weeks to come. They agreed to deal with the situation more thoroughly the next evening after supper, but that never happened.

The next day both parents were killed.

Some drunk crossed the centerline and hit them head-on, hurling them to deaths they neither expected nor deserved. Any teen would struggle with such senseless deaths, but this young lady carried an extra burden of unbearable proportions. She never had the chance to tell either her mother or father how sorry she was that she'd let them down, that she'd disobeyed them. The last time they'd spoken with her, all she'd heard was their displeasure. Never would she have the opportunity to hear again how much they loved her.

She mourned her sin. She wanted to put it behind her and forget it. If there ever was a penitent sinner, it was this girl. But because she couldn't express that penitence to the ones against whom she had sinned and because they couldn't respond with words and hugs of forgiveness, she couldn't *feel* the forgiveness she craved. It was as if the inability to confess to them somehow locked the guilt within her, taking away all avenues for removing it.

All she wanted was the chance to contritely confess and hear her parents reply, "We forgive you."

Confession Shines the Light of Healing on Sin

Confession—genuine, brokenhearted confession—unchains the sin from the recesses of our emotions and casts it into the light so that we can be healed. God legally forgives, even when we cannot yet face our actions—when we are not yet able to allow ourselves to feel shame and sorrow. But he wants to do more than legally forgive us. He also wants to heal our personal guilt. But our hearts only accept personal forgiveness when we face our shame and bring the sin openly to Him so that He can reassure us of our forgiveness.

Confession Confirms the Enormity of Sin

Confession gives us the avenue to make sure our sin is seen in its enormity so we can know our forgiveness is valid.

Allow me to explain.

If I stole money from you and later my guilt drove me to seek your forgiveness, I would want you to know how much money I actually stole. If you said, "Yes, stealing is an evil thing but I forgive you for taking the twenty dollars from my pocket," I would continue to feel guilty if I'd really stolen forty dollars. I would doubt the forgiveness unless I knew you understood the size of the sin.

I want forgiveness, but I also want the assurance that you know just how big a sin you are forgiving. I don't want to worry in the night that you will change your mind if you discover the reality of my sin.

I learned long ago that when Christians start to tell me of their sins, I do a disservice if I don't listen to the complete confession. Penitent people want to feel the guilt and be assured that I, the forgiver, feel it too. If I tell a fellow Christian a sin is inconsequential, I run the risk that person will think I don't understand and will subsequently discount any help for forgiveness that I offer.

Recently one of the godliest women in our church asked for prayers. She felt personal guilt for allowing her busy schedule to crowd out her time of personal Bible study and prayer. She didn't feel a "mild" personal guilt but a very strong personal guilt. As she confessed this sin to the brothers and sisters at church, tears flushed her cheeks, evidencing the shame she felt. She wanted us to understand her shame and pray with her for the spiritual strength and wisdom to reprioritize her life.

No sooner did the echoes of the closing prayer fade than a swarm of loving Christians surrounded her. They hugged, kissed, and cooed words of endearment. They spoke of her faith, her example, and her leadership. No one mentioned the sin causing her guilt. No one said, "I forgive you."

Later she shared with me the frustration of the experience. "By belittling my sin, they took away the very thing I sought. I didn't want to hear how good I am. I wanted them to hear and understand the guilt I felt. I sought healing. Not a 'pooh-poohing' of my sin. When will people realize that you can't emotionally accept their forgiveness if they don't emotionally accept your guilt?"

When a person confesses, it is with the hope that God and those sinned against will give healing for *all* the sin, not just a part of it.

Confession Allows Me to Feel Loved in Spite of My Sin

How does God reassure us that He loves us in spite of our sin and offers grace anyway? Through His Word, of course.

But how do we experience that love? We experience it through his children who know our sin and love us still. We can all read the Bible and see what God says about mercy and grace. But we may find that good news too wonderful to pull into our hearts. Our intellects agree with the truth of the Word; our emotions hold tight to the lie of our guilt.

When we carry the burden of unconfessed sin, no amount of praise or affection can soothe the pain in our hearts. Compliments bounce off; love can't penetrate. The unconfessed sin stands as a barrier to believing we are lovable, to believing we are worthwhile.

We think, "If they knew the truth about me, they wouldn't love me."

That's why we confess not only to God but also to other believers who can then apply the healing power of God's love and acceptance to our hurt.

If, after others know the whole truth about us, they still love us, the barrier to accepting God's forgiveness begins to come down. When we see that God's children can love us, in spite of our sin, we begin to believe that God can love us too. James said to handle sin like this: "Confess your sins to each other and pray for each other so that you may be healed. The prayer of a righteous man is powerful and effective."[4] This verse comes on the heels of James's exhortation for Christians to seek physical healing through the hands-on prayer of church elders.[5] Urging his "sick" brothers to call on righteous men for healing prayer, he adds that we should confess our sins to each other. Confession to godly people and their prayers concerning that confession lead to healing.

Confession Allows Me to Hear God's Message of Forgiveness

I know the truth and power of this passage because God used Jim Leek to tell me I was forgiven. He used Jim as a tool for my healing.

No. Jim didn't grant me legal forgiveness; God had already done that. But he started me on the road to personal forgiveness. Because he loved me as a brother in Christ, he had every right to help me on that journey.

He listened. He heard. He didn't whitewash or belittle. He felt my shame, and he gave me my cure. In a very real sense, he represented my Father in heaven who had waited for some time to speak those words to me. God spoke them through a gentle man with a keen mind, with the indwelling Spirit, with a strong shoulder and a tender touch.

Surely James contemplated a similar situation in his writings. He knew that godly men wouldn't castigate or cast out when they heard the sin story of a sick man. He knew they would correct if correction was needed, but above all they would pass on to the ill man the message of God: "I forgive you."

During the time of my physical problems, I continued to pray and study, but I found no relief. I found relief only when I confessed to a godly man (a man who happened to be an elder in the church, just like those James referenced) and he prayed for my healing, both spiritual and physical.

Confession Allows Fellow Believers to Diffuse the Power of Guilt

Years after Jim and I walked in the woods, he attended a three-day seminar we at Family Dynamics Institute conduct to train people to assist in strengthening and saving marriages. This time, I was the teacher and he the student. For two days, I watched a young minister in the group struggle with the guilt over a sin he'd committed, but for which he couldn't find healing. From a phone visit before he arrived, I knew some of the details of his sin, and I also knew he had stopped the sin. Following the example of my mentor, Jim, I didn't push. I just watched and waited. On the third day, the young man could take the pain of the shame no longer. Turning to the whole group, he blurted out his sin and the self-loathing it created. He spoke eloquent words, but the only emotion he showed was anger. When he finished, I asked, "Have you mourned your sin?"

"Oh, yes," he responded, "every day I feel bad for what I've done."

"No, I mean more than that. Have you cried over it?"

Of course he hadn't. "Real" men don't cry—especially ministers who are the strong helpers of others. When he finished his explanation, I looked to Jim. He was obviously reliving our front-porch experience just as I was. I nodded at him and he slowly came to his feet. He walked to the young minister and kneeled in front of him. Kindly, quietly, he looked into the young man's eyes and said, "I forgive you."

And I watched it happen all over again—this time as an observer rather than a participant. Finally, coming face to face with the emotions buried deep within him, the minister sobbed before Jesus. His confession before others accomplished in his heart what his confession before God had not. It shook the guilt free and flung it before two dozen godly people. It's power diffused, the guilt lost its hold over this young man.

We trampled it with love and refused to let him take it back.

God used us—specifically His servant Jim—to heal another guilt-caged Christian.

CONFESS AND BE HEALED

Is personal guilt tormenting you? Have you confessed it to God? If so, and if all the studies in this book haven't yet released you from it, it may be that you need to confess your sin to other godly people.

But choose these people wisely. After years of observation, I've noted that most Christians react to another Christian's sin in three basic ways:

> 1. If they recognize their own struggle with temptation in general and graciously accept the sacrifice of Jesus in payment for their sins, they tend to be gracious toward one who confesses sin.

2. If they never feel temptation toward the particular sin in question, they may tend to be critical, not understanding how anybody could do such a thing.
3. If they are tempted by the same sin but cannot admit it to themselves, they almost always become harsh and judgmental toward the confessing Christian.

It is, of course, the first kind of person to whom you want to confess. These people tend to be very grace-oriented when dealing with the sins of others. Even if they encounter a person struggling with a sin different from their own, they understand that sin is sin and that the temptation process is similar from one sin to another.

When searching for someone to talk to, be aware that some church leaders don't believe in mercy or grace. Their very dogma may force them to treat you badly, no matter how much they want to treat you with kindness. Look for people who live by grace, not by a system of law and works. And don't share your sin with gossips, power-mongers, egotists, or judges. Don't let anyone harangue and harass you until they make you reveal your innermost secrets. Godly people demonstrate fruit of the Spirit such as patience, kindness, and gentleness instead of fruit of the flesh such as jealousy, rage, and selfish ambition.[6]

Find good hearts who practice mercy and grace, people who will listen to your sin without passing it off as nothing or throwing you out of their house.

You know, people like Jesus.

There are a lot of them around. If you can't find one in your church, try the church down the street. If there isn't one there, try the church around the block. Don't think there aren't such people in your town just because they don't go to church with you. God has His people everywhere.

When you find those people, you may want to ask them to read this book before you share with them. At least make sure they know you are seeking spiritual healing. Ask them questions about their understanding of how God heals His children from personal sin. When you know you can trust them, open your heart and pour out your guilt. Don't hide, dress up, or slant anything to make you look good. Make sure you know they understand the enormity of the guilt eating you so that you can believe the forgiveness and healing they will by prayer and supplication help you seek.

Make sure they know how important it is to you to hear the words, "I forgive you." Tell them you can't hear it too often.

OVERCOME THREE FINAL BARRIERS TO SPIRITUAL HEALING

If you've followed all the teachings of this book, you should be well on your way to spiritual healing. There remain but three final barriers that must be removed in order to open yourself completely to the healing power of God.

> 1. You must forgive God.
> 2. You must forgive every human who has ever hurt you.
> 3. You must forgive yourself.

Forgive God

Among all the things I teach people, it seems that the idea of forgiving God receives one of the strongest reactions.

Those with a law/works mind-set jump on me with spurred boots when they hear it. "Give me book, chapter, and verse for that!" they cry. "You have no right to forgive God. God forgives you! What a blasphemous thing to tell Christians."

Of course, they are completely correct to tell me that no command of God supports my assertion. There is no scripture I know of that teaches me to forgive God. It is most certain that God neither needs nor requires my forgiveness. He's never sinned against me, and even if He could, I haven't the position or power to hold Him accountable.

But I'm not teaching a command of God when I tell you how to remove this last barrier to healing. I'm speaking as a human to other humans. I'm not asking you to forgive God because *He* needs it; I'm asking you to forgive God if *you* need to do it.

What do I mean when I ask you to forgive Him?

Not that you release Him from any legal guilt. He doesn't have any. Not that you forgive any sin. He's never committed one. Not that you forgive Him for violating your will. As any good parent, He follows the perfect way, not the whim of His children.

No, none of that.

I mean let go of the anger and hurt you feel toward Him, if you feel any at all. The first step is to tell Him what you feel. But the all-important next step is to then release your hurt. That's what I mean by forgiving God. You no longer hold Him responsible for the pain, no longer consider what He could have done differently for you.

If you are like thousands of other Christians with whom I've interacted over the years, there are likely times when you've felt anger toward God. Times when He stood silent though you begged for favor. Times when adversity or catastrophe clamored into your well-ordered Christian life, leaving you to wonder where God was when you needed Him. Times when you wanted Him to physically stop you, yet He allowed you to march into your own self-made hell.

Maybe like Martha and Mary you've chastised Jesus for not giving you the desire of your heart which you begged of Him.[7]

In faith you believe that God is sovereign and that He did the best thing for all involved, even if His reasoning is beyond the scope of your understanding. You refuse to become like the tycoon Ted Turner who, because his sister died, decided God doesn't exist. But you understand Ted's anger, and in those moments when you are most honest with yourself, you, too, feel a similar resentment toward God.

No, don't panic. That resentment, anger, or frustration doesn't jeopardize your salvation. God still saves you by His grace through your faith. But that resentment and hurt eat at you just as unhealed personal guilt does. It undermines God's actions designed to heal you. Finding emotional healing through the loving words of forgiveness from fellow Christians makes healing available. But any hidden anger toward God prevents its arrival.

You must look toward heaven and express your anger—not as a ritual of words, but as a catharsis, releasing pent-up and hidden emotions that prevent your relationship from being all God wants it to be.

Express your anger and unchain your pain. The Bible will tell you how. Surprised? Let's look again at King David. One of the things that has always impressed me about David is his openness and honesty with God. In the book of Psalms, David frequently expressed his frustration with God. Psalm 13 is a good example. Read how he begins:

> How long, O Lord? Will you forget me forever?
> How long will you hide your face from me?
> How long must I wrestle with my thoughts
> and every day have sorrow in my heart?

David doesn't fear venting his frustration and anger to God. He expresses his heart, not with disrespect, but with honesty—and David was a man after God's own heart.[8]

Besides being honest with God about even his negative emotions, David continued to work through his thoughts and feelings, and by the end of the psalm, he was singing a different tune. Listen to his conclusion:

> But I trust in your unfailing love;
>> my heart rejoices in your salvation.
> I will sing to the Lord,
>> for he has been good to me.

If David hadn't been writing by inspiration, we might question his quick change of heart—chastising God one moment and praising Him the next. It sounds like something a person would do who feared he'd gone too far in his complaint.

But not so with David. Obviously, something else happened. He released his anger. He let go of his hurt. He no longer held God responsible. He found peace in his heart by releasing his anger toward God.

I've seen many Christians do the same thing as they finally discover the healing of God. God heals them when they let go of their hurt or anger toward Him. May times I've witnessed a Christian reaching this point of release only when he or she could verbalize, "I forgive you, God, for letting it happen. I trust you enough to know that You did what should have been done, though I cannot understand it. Now, will You please forgive me for the emotions I've harbored against you?"

That prayer is never prayed without intense emotion.

And intense relief.

Several times throughout the Psalms[9] we see the pattern repeated. Frustration and anger vented—praises offered to God—a return to trust in God. The pattern can work for you too.

1. Honestly and openly express your anger and frustration to God.
2. After a period of venting, turn your efforts toward praising God for the good things He has done for you and for who He is.
3. Speak words of trust and faith; tell God that you trust Him to heal you of your anger.
4. Give God time to work on your heart, repeating the first three steps as needed.

When Martha and Mary chastised Jesus, He offered no defense, admonition, or punishment. He didn't respond negatively at all. In fact, He wept with them.[10]

Forgive Those Who've Hurt You

Jesus pointed out the second barrier to receiving the healing of God. "If you forgive men when they sin against you, your heavenly Father will also forgive you. But if you do not forgive men their sins, your Father will not forgive your sins."[11]

Remember the verses we studied from 1 John, the ones that said that those who love walk in the light? Well, 1 John also teaches that those who hate live in darkness. Jesus and the inspired authors of the New Testament visited that theme often. We can't claim to live in the light, to have living, saving faith and yet continue to live in hatred. Hatred prevents faith from ever taking root. Or it kills faith that doesn't have deep enough roots.

Love is a sign that faith is alive and we are saved. Hate is a sign that faith is nonexistent and we are lost. That's what John said.

If you carry hatred in your heart for people who have hurt you in your life, you carry the seeds of death within you. It may be that you're struggling. That's okay. Weak faith receives just as much grace as strong faith. But it will never be enough to gain God's healing. You must release your hatred and extend forgiveness instead.

I recall meeting a man years ago whose only purpose for living was to kill the man who murdered his daughter. The hatred consumed him, destroying his faith, deadening his spirit. He had no use for God or people. All he wanted was vengeance.

One woman showed me the gun she carried in her purse that she wanted to use on the relative who had sexually abused her as a child. She wanted to kill him, yet she wanted to be a Christian. The dichotomy spiraled her into deep spiritual depression.

I've watched others stand behind pulpits or hide behind editorial desks and spew hatred and rage at those who disagree with them. They evidence no countenance of peace nor do they show any fruit of the Spirit in their lives. Their hatred makes them worse than any sin they imagine in their victims. They shrivel spiritually and stare blankly when someone talks of God healing Christians of their guilt.

I know what I'm talking about. I entered the most sinful period of my life propelled by the anger and unforgiving spirit I felt toward brothers who had hurt me. I spoke of the grace of God and taught it clearly, even while it was slipping beyond my own understanding. My inability to forgive led me into a spiritual state where I couldn't find God at all. I knew my sin, both legally and personally, but I didn't have the spiritual strength to find God so He could remove my guilt.

Refusing to forgive can destroy you.

It will, at the least, keep you from reaching the healed spiritual state you desire.

Now would be a good time to take a pad of paper and write out all the hurt you've received from people and have been unable to forgive. As soon as you finish this book, spend several days in prayer, asking God to show you any hatred, anger, or lack of forgiveness residing in you. As it is revealed, write it down. Write the name of the person, the nature of the offense, and what you feel about it. Make it as detailed as possible; pour your emotions onto the paper.

When you're sure you are done, take the notebook before God in prayer. Ask Him to heal each hurt; specify your hurt and what you feel. Tell God what you wish to feel instead. Ask Him to replace every negative emotion toward each of the names in your notebook with a Christian emotion for that person. Pray regularly about your hurts—every day if you can—and watch God work. Two things will happen with a little time. The first is that you will find your resentment, anger, and hatred dissipating and being replaced by Christian love. The second is that you'll discover that the healing you've been seeking will become yours.

You may find that you need to visit with some of the folks on your list.[12] If that happens, don't be afraid. Follow God and watch Him heal more than you ever thought possible.

Forgive Yourself

Perhaps the most common lament I hear is: "I just can't forgive myself for what I've done. Can you tell me how I can forgive me?"

If a person asks that from a human standpoint, I don't know the answer. Various psychologists have tried various things. Some try to get you to revisit the event in your memory and act it out again, this time doing the right thing. Others tell you to write in a diary at the end of each day, describing the events as they should have happened rather than how they did. Still others try to remove the event from active memory by hypnosis. Some insist it wasn't your fault and help you figure out who to blame. And some just write prescriptions so that one sip of water washes down a medical miracle and makes everything new.

But none of that works very effectively.

I believe the answer is spiritual. We discussed it in chapter 6: It is believing what God tells you about you; it is refusing to see yourself through any human eyes—even your own—and seeing yourself through the eyes of God instead. *Forgiving yourself is really just accepting God's forgiveness of you.*

You've heard the old saying about wearing rose-tinted glasses. It refers to people who refuse to see the world as it is and put their own tint on it so it appears more beautiful. Well, I wear God-tinted glasses now. I refuse to see what I have done; I see me as God sees me through the Son. If the Greatest Being in existence, the God who knows me better than I know myself, sees me as forgiven, I am a fool to see myself in any other way.

God knows how many hairs are on my head. I don't. He can see what I will do tomorrow. I can't. He knows things I do that don't even register on my consciousness—ignorant sins and unintentional sins. He knows the selfish emotions that drive me to sin, even when I disguise them from myself so I won't feel even worse about myself. He knows the weaknesses I refuse to acknowledge. He knows the pain I don't admit to myself. He knows me in every possible way.

And He still forgives me.

Since He can forgive me, it is ludicrous for me not to forgive myself, not to believe I am forgiven.

The same is true of you.

You haven't hurt yourself more than you've hurt God. You haven't let anyone down more than you've disappointed Him. You haven't exposed your darkest, vilest moments to anyone like you have to Him.

And He still forgives you. Do you believe that now?

If so, it's time to forgive yourself.

Ready?

Find a mirror. Look the sinner—you—right in the eye. Listen as you tell yourself how sinful you are and what shame you feel.

Then forgive yourself.

Tell yourself, "I forgive you."

If you've followed all the counsel in this book, you already have the forgiveness of God. He, through His word, has already said, "I forgive you." You've also sought the healing touch of godly people. You've confessed your sin before them, and they've said, "I forgive you." Now you've stood in front of a mirror and said to yourself, "I forgive you." I ask you the same question Jesus asked the woman caught in adultery, "Where are they? Has no one condemned you?"[13]

And, of course, you will answer, "No one, sir."[14]

Jesus says to you, "Then neither do I condemn you. . . . Go now and leave your life of sin."[15]

He knows you. He knows what you've done. And He knows what He's talking about.

Believe Him and be healed.

QUESTIONS

Introduction

1. Why do you think the "grandmotherly" woman whose story began this chapter continued to struggle with guilt for so many years?

2. Think of people you know—perhaps even yourself—who have struggled with guilt. List everything you can think of that caused their struggles with guilt.

3. What do you think "forgiven forever" means?

4. What would you have advised the woman in this Introduction to do to overcome her guilt?

Chapter 1: What Good Is Guilt?

1. Read Isaiah 57:15–19 and give a brief definition of these concepts found there: revival, comfort, peace, direction, and healing.

2. What do you think it means to be healed of sin and not just forgiven of it?

3. How would a person know that he is not a spiritual sociopath?

4. "Afterlust" is mentioned under the heading "Satan Reminds You of Your Past." What is afterlust? Why does it occur? What does it communicate to the Christian who experiences it?

5. This chapter lists several methods that satanic forces use to make "spiritual cripples" of Christians. Which of these methods have you seen used against you? Which have you seen used on others? How were they used?

6. If you had been Marshall Underwood, what would you have done?

7. Give a brief description of a time in your life—or in the life of someone you know—when God used guilt for good.

8. What do you think is the most important point made in this chapter?

Chapter 2: Where Does Guilt Come From?

1. Before you read this chapter, how would you have answered this question: "If guilt is such a strong motivator to repent, why isn't it just as strong a motivator to stop a Christian from sinning?" How would you answer it now?

2. In your own words explain *unintentional sin* and give examples (besides those in the chapter) of how a person could commit each of the two kinds of unintentional sin.

3. In your own words explain *ignorant sin* and give an example (different from those found in the chapter).

4. Why does God note legal guilt for sins that people don't even know they did or that they did unintentionally?

5. Why is it important to understand the difference in legal guilt and personal guilt?

6. Why is intentional sin always arrogant, no matter what the circumstance or situation?

7. Give examples of how a person could be in the deceived spiritual state.

8. Why does a person in the aware spiritual state *have* to act?

9. Why would a person in the aware spiritual state ever move back into the deceived spiritual state?

10. What does the concept of being "healed of sin and guilt" mean to you?

Chapter 3: How Does Guilt Affect Me?

1. Explain the difference between mind, body, and spirit.
2. How can sin and guilt confuse your reasoning (your heart)? (Read endnote 7 for this chapter for ideas.)
3. Under the heading "Reasoning," three results of guilt confusion are mentioned. Give a brief explanation of each.
4. How can guilt affect a person's body?
5. As best you can, describe what a human spirit is.
6. How does sin and guilt affect the relationship between God's Spirit and a person's spirit?
7. What did you learn when you did the prayer and meditation exercise under "The Spirit" heading?
8. What insight into sin or guilt did you get from this study on the trinary nature of mankind?

Chapter 4: Why Do I Sin?

1. What was your reaction when you read at the beginning of this chapter that a church allowed a recovering alcoholic to serve as a deacon? Why?
2. The King James Version translates *sarx* as "flesh," and the New International Version translates it as "sinful nature." Which translation do you think better explains what *sarx* is? Can you think of a better way to translate it?
3. Explain the flesh's three self-directed drives.
4. Why can't you overcome all temptation just by disciplining your mind?
5. The author describes "The Process of Mind Defeat" that leads to sin. Briefly outline that process. Using that outline, write a one-paragraph story of a person yielding to a specific temptation.
6. How do satanic forces tempt Christians into repetitive sins?

7. How could a person become addicted to a sin?

8. How does sin contaminate every part of us—body, mind, and spirit?

9. In a book on forgiveness, why should an entire chapter be devoted to studying temptation and sin?

10. What did you think was the most important point in this chapter?

Chapter 5: What Can I Do to Stop Feeling Guilty?

1. What is repressed guilt?

2. What is restitution for sin? Give at least two examples.

3. Why doesn't restitution remove all guilt?

4. What is contrition for sin? Give an example.

5. Why doesn't contrition remove all guilt?

6. What is spiritual balancing? Give at least two examples.

7. How does a person who attempts spiritual balancing to remove guilt inadvertently replace God by that act?

8. What is confession for sin? Give an example.

9. Why doesn't confession automatically move one into the healed spiritual state?

10. How can restitution, contrition, balancing, and confession all be part of the path to spiritual healing but not the destination?

Chapter 6: Believe What God Tells You about You

1. How does it make you feel to realize that the power to stop sinning does not come from your mind or spirit? Where does it come from?

2. Read Psalm 51:7 and Psalm 103:12. What do these verses tell you about how God removes Christians' guilt?

3. Explain why you agree or disagree with this statement from this chapter: "God kills your guilt in the legal annals of heaven when you are His."

4. Explain why you agree or disagree with this statement from this chapter: "God kills your guilt in your heart, mind, and spirit when you believe Him that it is dead." What is the difference in this statement and the one in the previous question?

5. What does God mean when He tells us that our "old self" is crucified with Jesus?

6. How is the removal of personal guilt tied directly to our acceptance of and belief in the crucifixion of our old self?

7. Explain Romans 8:5–9.

8. What are the two diseases that result from not believing that God removes your sin and guilt?

9. What did you think was the most important point in this chapter?

Chapter 7: Believe That Mercy and Grace Are Yours

1. Explain Ephesians 2:8–9.

2. What is a law/works system of salvation?

3. How does Galatians 3:10–11 show that no one will be saved by a law/works system?

4. Give an example (other than those in the book) of how someone might rationalize disobeying "optional" laws as long as they obey "essential" laws. What is wrong with this kind of reasoning?

5. How does trusting in a law/works system of salvation affect a person's relationship with God?

6. How could a person use the godly act of confession as part of a law/works system?

7. Why did God give us a law we can't keep?

8. What is the important point about our salvation that we learn from God's justifying Abraham *before* his circumcision because of his faith?

9. How could a person be an active, obedient church member and not be a Christian?

10. Define *grace* and *mercy*. What is the difference? How do they affect your relationship with God?

Chapter 8: Believe God's Assurances

1. What is God wanting to convince us of in 1 John 5:13?

2. Explain 1 John 1:7. What does it say about when a Christian is forgiven?

3. List all the advantages that would come from having Jesus as your "defense attorney" if you were on trial for your sins.

4. How is it that we are saved by *faith* if God commands us to *obey* Him?

5. How does God assure us of our salvation in 1 John 2:9–10?

6. How can Christians know if they love their brothers and sisters?

7. Tell why you agree or disagree with the author's statement that to see if our faith is alive we should look for "direction" and not "perfection."

8. Why do Christians' hearts sometimes "condemn" them, as mentioned in 1 John 3:19–20? What does John say we should do when our hearts condemn us? Why?

9. What is the difference in sensitivity to sin and doubting one's salvation?

10. Why does God bountifully answer the prayers of His children, even though they continually struggle with sin?

Chapter 9: Answer Satan's Lies with God's Truths

1. How can Christians get beyond the barrier of believing they don't deserve God's forgiveness?

2. What does "taking the fifth" before God mean? Why should we take comfort in it?

3. Why is grieving for an abandoned sin a human reaction that shouldn't surprise us?

4. How can Christians keep their sin-grief from becoming a tool of Satan?

5. Give examples of how you've seen Satan's forces use unforgiving people to try to make forgiven sinners doubt their forgiveness.

6. How do distorted views of God keep people from believing God loves them? What kind of distorted views?

7. Explain Romans 5:8 in terms of what it says to sinners doubting that they are forgiven.

Chapter 10: Confess and Be Healed

1. Explain 1 John 1:9 in light of 1 John 1:7.

2. Why would God forgive a Christian who sins *before* the Christian confesses to Him and asks Him to forgive?

3. How does confession "remove the barrier within" so that we can be healed of personal guilt?

4. Why do we want the people from whom we ask forgiveness to understand the enormity of our sin and the guilt we feel?

5. List ways that Christians sometimes downplay the seriousness of the guilt felt by a confessing Christian. Why do you think they do that? What specific things should they do instead?

6. The author lists three reactions Christians sometimes have to another Christian's sin. Briefly explain each of these reactions as you understand them.

7. Why is it so important to say "I forgive" when responding to a confessing Christian?

8. Why would a person ever need to forgive God?

9. What happened as you made your list of people who had hurt you or toward whom you held negative feelings and then prayed for God to heal the hurt?

10. Why does the act of forgiving the person who sinned against you set you free? How does it accomplish that? Does it also set the sinner free?

11. What is the most important thing you learned from reading this book?

NOTES

My Story

1. Joe Beam, *Seeing the Unseen* (West Monroe, La.: Howard Publishing, 1994).

Introduction

1. Joe Beam, *Forgiven Forever* (West Monroe, La.: Howard Publishing, 1994), videocassette.

Chapter 1. What Good Is Guilt?

1. Isa. 57:15–19.
2. Heb. 13:4.
3. Matt. 23:27–28.
4. 2 Pet. 2:14.
5. John 8:44.
6. 1 Cor. 2:11.
7. 1 Sam. 16:7; Acts 15:8.
8. 1 Tim. 4:1–4.
9. This is a direct violation of 1 Corinthians 7:12–13, but they seemed not to care. They apparently believed that if he didn't concur that they alone were saved, and if he continued to meet with another church, then she shouldn't live with him. They encouraged the divorce, and even helped hide his children from him until he regained custody by a court order.

10. This is a clear violation of 1 Corinthians 7:1–5. The couple continued to live in the same house but without conjugal relations. The way they were emotionally able to accomplish this difficult task was to become enemies. They never divorced, and they lived together for many years before their respective deaths. In all the time I knew them, neither ever said a kind word about the other. At each funeral, I silently asked myself how much different their lives would have been if Satan's forces, using the erroneous teachings of their church leaders, hadn't been able to destroy the love between this husband and wife.

11. Rom. 6:1.

Chapter 2. Where Does Guilt Come From?

1. Lev. 4:2.
2. Lev. 5:14–16.
3. Exod. 20:7
4. Matt. 5:28
5. Lev. 5:17–19.
6. 1 John 3:4.
7. Acts 9:1.
8. Acts 23:1.
9. 1 Cor. 4:4.
10. Lev. 6:1–7.
11. Rom. 2:22.
12. Rom. 6:23.
13. Rom. 13:9.
14. Mal. 2:16.
15. John 16:8.
16. Ps. 51:17.
17. Acts 8:39.
18. Heb. 10:22.
19. Heb. 3:12.
20. Isa. 57:15–19.
21. 1 John 2:1.
22. Eph. 2:10.

23. Rom. 4:7–8.

24. Gal. 6:7.

Chapter 3. How Does Guilt Affect Me?

1. Heb. 2:14.

2. Mark 5:15.

3. Zech. 12:1; Eccles. 12:7.

4. Watchman Nee employed a similar model in *Releasing the Spirit*. In his model he used *soul* where I use *mind*. Apparently, several people use the same terminology as Nee and prefer soul to mind in this context. While mind and soul are not always interchangeable, many of the concepts used by Nee and others for *soul* fit well into *mind* as I use it. One basic difference is that Nee calls the body the "outer man" (with which I agree), the soul the "inner man," and the spirit the "inmost man." It seems to me that, at least in the New International Version, both "inner man" and "inmost man" refer to the spirit.

5. Those in the first century saw the heart as the place where the emotions and intellect came together into a center of reasoning. Many passages use *heart* to mean the combination of intellect and emotion. (e.g. Matt. 5:8, Matt. 6:21, Luke 6:45, Acts 2:37, Col. 3:23, Heb. 4:12.) Occasionally Bible writers separated the *heart* from the *mind* when they wanted to make a point about involving every nuance of our being (e.g. Luke 10:27, Acts 4:32). But most of the time they used *heart* to refer to the combination of intellect and emotions. For example, in Matthew 13:15, Jesus said, "They . . . see with their eyes, hear with their ears, understand with their hearts and turn." In this verse, "heart" includes understanding and emotion. In Romans 10:10 it's even clearer: "For it is with your heart that you believe and are justified." Here, "heart" obviously includes more than just emotion and more than just intellect.. Faith is trust placed in Jesus, and it is with the "heart" that we place our trusting faith in Him. Unless you think of faith as a dry, intellectual acknowledgment, you will agree that "heart" in this passage means both intellect and emotions.

Therefore, to New Testament writers, "guarding the heart" (Phil. 4:7) meant guarding the combined intellect and emotions so that a person reasoned correctly and acted accordingly.

6. Luke 5:8.

7. The heart's confusion comes as it acknowledges the pleasure it feels from the sin committed while also recognizing the personal guilt produced by that sin. If both feelings are strong, your heart becomes unable to reason properly, disconcerted by the perplexity of powerful emotions at war within you. Your intellect, feeble against such strong emotions, often loses its power to influence your reasoning. As a result, your heart usually yields to the emotion felt most keenly.

When that happens one of three things will occur:

1. If feelings of guilt or fear are more powerful than the pleasure of sin, you flee the temptation.

2. If the pleasure of the sin overpowers the guilt and fear you feel, your emotions lead you dully back to the place or person of sin.

3. If guilt at first overcomes the pleasure but then subsides too rapidly, the temptation comes again. Satan's forces wait for guilt to lose its persuasion, then skillfully return.

If either of the latter two occur, guilt confuses the heart even more.

8. Luke 6:41.

9. That's apparently what drove King David to order the execution of a man he thought to have mistreated a neighbor while he himself stood guilty of "bloodguilt": for adultry and murder (Ps. 51:14).

10. Ps. 51:5.

11. Ps. 51:3.

12. Ps. 51:11.

13. Heb. 4:12.

14. Ps. 32:3.

15. Ps. 51:8.

16. Prov. 14:30.

17. Prov. 15:13.

18. Proverbs 17:22.

19. Rom. 5:12, 17.

20. John 4:24

21. Gen. 1:26; 5:1.

22. Prov. 20:27.

23. Isa. 26:9.

24. Ps. 103:1.

25. James 2:26, cf. Luke 8:25.

26. 1 Cor. 2:11.

27. Eph. 3:16.

28. 1 Cor. 2:6–16.

29. 1 Cor. 6:17.

30. Ps. 51:10–12.

31. Ps. 51:11.

32. Ps. 34:18.

33. Ps. 51:17.

34. Isa. 57:15.

35. Rom. 7:5.

36. James 5:13–16.

Chapter 4. Why Do I Sin?

1. In my book, *Seeing the Unseen,* also from Howard Publishing, chapters 11 and 12 deal extensively with temptation and sin. I won't repeat that information here, but I do recommend that book if you want to study this subject in greater depth.

2. William F. Arndt and F. Wilbur Gingrich, *A Greek-English Lexicon of the New Testament and Other Early Christian Literature* (n.p.: The University of Chicago Press, 1957), p. 751.

3. Luke 24:39.

4. Gal. 5:17.

5. Matt. 6:25–34.

6. Rom. 7:15–19.

7. Rom. 7:18.

8. Rom. 7:23.

9. Rom. 7:5.

10. Rom. 12:2.

11. Col. 3:2.

12. Rom. 1:28.

13. Matt. 16:23.

14. Matt. 16:22.

15. 2 Sam. 11:2.

16. 2 Sam. 11:14–26.

17. 2 Sam. 12:15–18.

18. 2 Sam. 13:1–21.

19. 2 Sam. 13:23–37.

20. 2 Sam. 18:1–8.

21. 2 Cor. 7:1.

22. 1Thess. 5:23.

23. 1 John 1:8.

24. Rom. 7:25.

Chapter 5. What Can I Do to Stop Feeling Guilty?

1. Actually, that would be impossible under Old Testament law. If a woman was divorced by one husband and married another, she could never remarry the first husband again (Deut. 24:1–4).

2. Rom. 6:23.

3. Ps. 34:18.

4. Eph. 2:8–9.

5. Eph. 2:10.

6. James 5:16.

Chapter 6. Believe What God Tells You about You

1. Rom. 7:24.

2. Rom. 7:25.

3. Rom. 5:8.

4. Matt. 26:39.

5. 2 Cor. 5:17.

6. Luke 19:10.

7. 2 Pet. 3:9.

8. 2 Cor. 5:21.

9. Ps. 103:12.

10. Ps. 51:7.

11. John 3:6–7.

12. Luke 5:8.

13. Luke 5:10.

14. Rom. 6:7.

15. 2 Cor. 5:17.

16. Lev. 16:10.

17. For example, in His new resurrection body, He could walk through walls (John 20:26) or change His appearance (Luke 24:13–31).

18. Rom. 6:6–7.

19. Rom. 6:8.

20. Rom. 6:11.

21. John R. W. Stott, *Men Made New, An Exposition of Romans 5–8* (n.p.: Intervarsity Press, 1966), pp. 49–51.

22. Heb. 11:6.

23. 1 Cor. 6:9–11.

24. Rom. 8:2.

25. Rom. 8:4.

26. Rom. 8:5–9.

27. Acts 2:38; 5:32.

28. 1 Pet. 2:24.

Chapter 7. Believe That Mercy and Grace Are Yours

1. Luke 7:39.

2. Luke 7:44.

3. Luke 7:47.

4. Luke 7:48.

5. Luke 7:50.

6. Gal. 3:10–11.

7. Matt. 15:5–9.

8. Phil. 2:13.

9. Gal. 3:19.

10. Ibid.

11. Gal. 3:24.

12. Acts 13:39.

13. Gal. 3:21–22.

14. Rom. 6:23.

15. Rom. 4:2–5.

16. Rom. 4:10.

17. Rom. 4:11.

18. Rom. 4:13.

19. Eph. 2:8–9.

20. Gal. 3:10.

21. Gal. 1:9.

22. 1 John 2:1.

Chapter 8. Believe God's Assurance

1. 1 John 5:13. The other four purposes stated are (1) that we may have fellowship (1:3); (2) that we may have joy (1:4); (3) that we may not sin (2:1); and (4) that we may not be deceived (2:26).

2. 1 John 1:7.

3. 2 Cor. 5:21.

4. Rom. 6:23.

5. 2 Cor. 5:14.

6. 1 John 2:1a.

7. Rom. 3:12.

8. 1 John 2:1b.

9. Arndt and Gingrich, *Greek-English Lexicon of the New Testament and Other Early Christian Literature*, p. 623.

10. Rom. 6:3–4.

11. Matt. 25:21.

12. 1 John 2:3.

13. 1 John 5:4.

14. James 2:17.

15. James 2:24.

16. James 2:26.

17. See Galatians, Ephesians 2, and Romans, especially chapter 4.

18. James 1:25.

19. James 2:24.

20. Rom. 4.

21. James 1:21.

22. James 1:22.

23. James 1:23.

24. Rom. 4:23–24.

25. James 2:24.

26. 1 John 2:10.

27. 1 John 3:16–18.

28. Matt. 26:39.

29. Matt. 14: 13–23.

30. Matt. 19:13–15.

31. 1 John 3:19–20.

32. 1 John 4:13.

33. 2 Cor. 1:22.

34. Eph. 1:13–14.

35. Luke 7:36–50.

36. 1 John 4:17–18.

37. 1 John 5:14–15.

38. James 5:17.

39. 1 Kings 18:40.

40. 1 Kings 19:1–10.

41. Yes, it is absolutely true that God blesses prayers given in absolute faith (Matt. 21:22). But I'm not suggesting here that a weakened Christian's prayer carries the same efficacy as the petition of a prayer warrior. I'm saying that God *does* answer the prayer of the struggling or weak Christian. The very fact that He answers evidences that the struggler still has a father/child relationship with the heavenly Father.

42. James 4:3.

43. Luke 11:29.

44. Judges 6:37–40.

Chapter 9. Answer Satan's Lies with God's Truth

1. 2 Thess. 1:7–9.
2. Rev. 21:8 KJV.
3. Luke 15:21.
4. Rom. 5:6.
5. Rom. 5:8.
6. Rom. 5:20.
7. 2 Sam. 12:13.
8. Matt. 5:23–24.
9. Luke 15:11–31.
10. Rom. 5:6–8.

Chapter 10. Confess and Be Healed

1. See chapter 3, pages 63–64.
2. See chapter 6, pages 117–121.
3. 1 John 1:9.
4. James 5:16.
5. James 5:14–15.
6. Gal. 5:22–23.
7. John 11:21, 32.
8. 1 Sam. 13:14.
9. Pss. 4, 10, 22, 64, 142.
10. John 11:35.
11. Matt. 6:14–15.
12. Matt. 8:15–16.
13. John 8:10.
14. John 8:11.
15. Ibid.

Family Dynamics

Just as I started work on this book, God opened the doors of heaven and gave me the opportunity to found Family Dynamics Institute. I could write an entire book about how God has used and is using FDI in absolutely astounding ways. As the name of our nonprofit organization implies, FDI works with families—most often in marriage relationships or parent/child relationships—across the USA and Canada. God uses the seminars and courses He gave us to bring amazing results in several areas of family life. We are tremendously successful in re-creating love and intimacy in couples who've lost those feeling for each other. We're just as effective in dramatically deepening those emotions in couples who already have wonderful relationships, making their bond of love stronger than they ever thought possible. We have opened the eyes of parents to see how their parenting behaviors affect their children and why their children act and react as they do. We then help them learn to parent their children as God parents us.

Quite a wonderful ministry, isn't it? And it's still growing. We're slowly expanding around the world. Hundreds of churches now use our interactive seminars and courses with hundreds more learning about us each year. Our growth continues to be exponential, and we come to work everyday excited to see what God has done and has in store for us to do to bless more families.

If you would like to know more about how Family Dynamics can bless your marriage, your family, or your church, please contact us for more information. Write us at P.O. Box 211668, Augusta, GA 30917-1668 or call us at 1-800-650-9995.

FAMILY DYNAMICS SEMINARS

His Needs, Her Needs

This is our basic interactive seminar, using the book *His Needs, Her Needs* as a resource. This course provides direction, principles, and tools to help any marriage be better. Couple who go through this course become closer to one another and develop a renewed commitment to their marriage. This course is changing lives.

Love, Sex, & Marriage

This exciting weekend course is fast-paced, fun, and upbeat. It usually begins on Friday evening and continues through Saturday. Couples in your church will love what they learn about making their marriages wonderful and will have a great time learning it. The presentation is humorous, touching, and powerful. Using Bible exposition and real-life stories, we make strong, practical applications for everyday married life.

JOE BEAM REVIVALS

Joe Beam captivates audiences. That is one of the reasons that churches around the world invite him to speak in revivals. Though dedicated to his work at Family Dynamics, he reserves several weeks each year just for the purpose of revival among churches. He usually speaks twice on Sunday morning (Bible class and worship) and each evening, Sunday through Tuesday.

Spiritual Warfare Revival

Typically, when this revival is offered, coupled with Joe's presentation based on his book, *Seeing the Unseen,* the building is filled at each service. Sinners find salvation. Christians find a renewed dependence upon God. Topics include:

- Spirits, Angels, and Demons in Our World
- The Plan of the Silver-Tongued Devil
- The Forces at Work against Us
- The Forces at Work for Us

Joe discusses sin, temptation, and deliverance. He leads the audience through a biblical understanding of why bad things happen to good people and how God gives the final victory.

Intimacy with God

Using material shared in this book, Joe leads audiences to understand intellectually and emotionally the forgiveness of God and the healing He offers. From there, he leads them into a study of what it means to walk by the Spirit every day.

For information about any speaking engagement, contact Joe at P.O. Box 211440, Augusta, GA 30917-1440.